The 500 Hidden Secrets

of **FLANDERS FIELDS** *and*

the **BELGIAN COAST**

INTRODUCTION

This is a guide to hidden places in Ypres and the battlefields of
Flanders, as well as some secret spots along the Belgian coast. The aim
is to take you through the streets of Ypres and Poperinge in search of
haunting relics of the First World War, and to guide you through the
beautiful countryside around Ypres in search of the small museums,
lost cemeteries and secret remnants of a global conflict.
Now is the perfect moment to visit this region, since many of the
war sites have been improved and upgraded for the 100th anniversary of the war. There are outstanding new visitors' centres, along with
walking trails, cycle routes, good restaurants and cool B&Bs.

The aim of this guide is to inspire you and guide you to some of the
less well visited places in the region. You do not have to do everything listed here, but you should try to visit one or two cemeteries,
spend a couple of hours in one of the museums and take a walk
along one of the battlefield trails. You will then begin to understand
the history of this tragic and yet beautiful region of Europe.
The book doesn't mention every battle or military detail. There are
already more than enough excellent guides to the battlefields. This
book goes beyond traditional guides to include places that are not in
any way connected to the war, like the Flemish foodie restaurants,
local breweries and cool design shops.

The section on the Belgian coast aims to take you away from the
overcrowded parts and find the hidden places where you can eat
excellent seafood, discover quirky little museums, hike in windswept
dunes and sleep in fabulous B&Bs.

HOW TO USE
THIS BOOK?

This book contains 500 things about Ypres, Flanders Fields and the
Belgian Coast in 100 different categories. Some are places to visit.
Others are random bits of information. The aim is to inspire you to go
beyond the obvious tourist sites, not to cover everything from A to Z.

The places in this guide are given an address, a town or village, and
a region. The region refers to one of the maps at the front of the
book. These maps indicate the main towns and villages listed in
the guide. The maps are designed to give you an overview, but they
aren't detailed enough to navigate around. You can find up-to-date
maps on the internet, or pick up a free map at your hotel or the local
tourist office.

You need to bear in mind that places change all the time. The chef
who hits a high note one day can be uninspiring on the day you
happen to visit. The hotel ecstatically reviewed in this book might
suddenly go downhill under a new manager. The bar considered one
of the best places in Ostend for live music might be empty on the
night you turn up.

This is obviously a highly personal selection. You might not always
agree with it. If you want to leave a comment, recommend a bar or
reveal your favourite secret place, you can contact the publisher at
info@lusterweb.com.

THE AUTHOR

Derek Blyth has lived in Belgium for more than 20 years. As a journalist, he has explored almost every corner of the country. He has visited Ypres and Flanders Fields many times and explored each of the 13 resorts along the Belgian coast.

Formerly editor of the Brussels English-language weekly The Bulletin, he has written several books on the Low Countries, including three books in the *500 Hidden Secrets* series on Brussels, Antwerp and Ghent.

In drawing up this list of 500 hidden secrets, the author has taken advice from friends, family and neighbours, as well as Belgian journalists and local historians. He is especially grateful to Christa Deplacie, Diederik Vandenbilcke, Karin De Bruyn, Dettie Luyten and Hadewijch Ceulemans for their tips.

The author has some favourite spots in Flanders Fields where he likes to return, like the forgotten German cemetery at Vladslo on a misty winter morning, the Lone Tree Cemetery on Messines Ridge at dusk and the Dolle Brouwers café on a Sunday afternoon. He also likes certain spots on the Belgian coast, like the corner table in Café Du Parc in Ostend, the little ferry at Nieuwpoort and the windswept dunes at Oostduinkerke. This book is an attempt to share his enthusiasms with the reader.

FLANDERS FIELDS *and* *the* BELGIAN COAST

overview

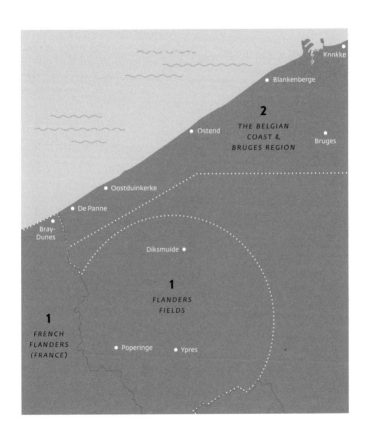

Map 1
FLANDERS FIELDS
& FRENCH FLANDERS

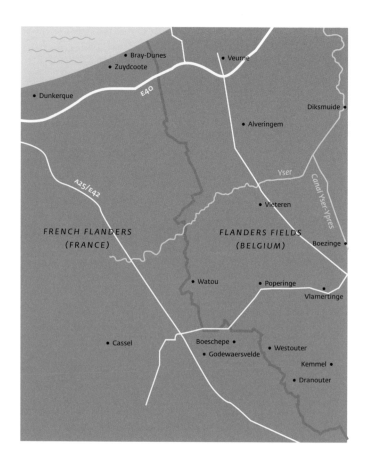

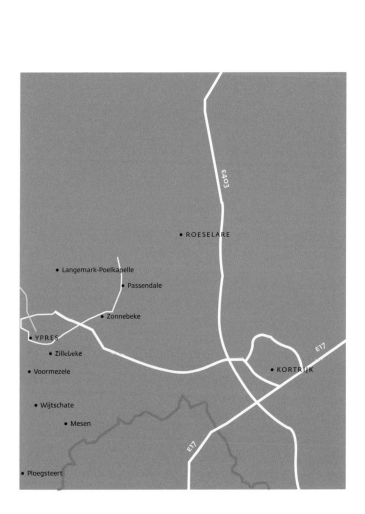

Map 2
THE BELGIAN COAST
& BRUGES REGION

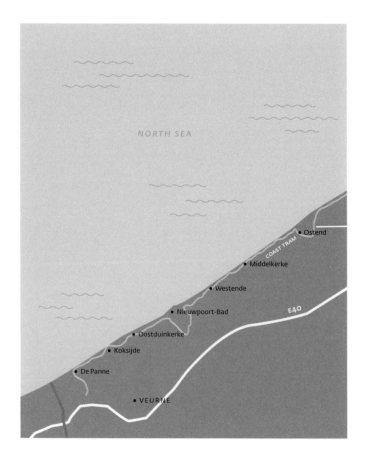

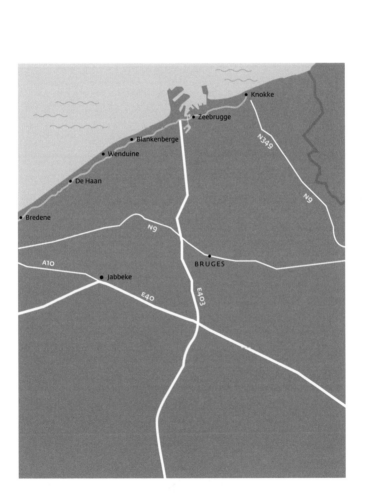

SOUVENIR

85 PLACES
TO EAT GOOD FOOD

The 5 places for **GOOD FOOD** *in Ypres* —————— 14

The 5 most **ROMANTIC RESTAURANTS**
in Ypres ———————————————————— 16

The 5 best places to eat in **FLANDERS FIELDS** — 19

The 5 best **POPERINGE AND**
DIKSMUIDE *restaurants* ————————— 21

The 5 most appealing **COUNTRY INNS**
in French Flanders ———————————— 23

The 5 best places for **CREATIVE COOKING**
at the coast ————————————————— 25

The 5 best places for **FRESH FISH**
FROM THE NORTH SEA ———————— 27

The 5 best restaurants for **A STEAMING POT**
OF MUSSELS ————————————————— 29

The 5 **COOLEST PLACES TO EAT**
at the coast —————————————— 32

The 5 best places for **SERIOUS STEAKS
AND BURGERS** —————————————— 34

The 5 best places to eat
SHRIMP CROQUETTES ———————— 36

The 5 best places for **CHEAP EATS** ———————— 38

The 5 best shops for **BELGIAN CHOCOLATES** — 40

The 5 best places for **ICE CREAM** ———————— 42

The 5 best **FISH MARKETS
AND FISHMONGERS** ———————————— 44

The 5 **SPECIALITIES TO EAT
IN THE WESTHOEK** ———————————— 46

The 5 **SPECIALITIES OF
THE BELGIAN COAST** ———————————— 48

The 5 places for
GOOD FOOD
in Ypres

---

1 **SOUVENIR**
Surmont
de Volsbergestraat 12
Ypres
Flanders Fields
+32 (0)57 36 06 06
*www.souvenir-
restaurant.be*

This is a stylish restaurant with a modern Scandinavian interior of white walls and pale wood. Not like Ypres at all. The young Icelandic chef Vilhjalmur Sigurdarson used to work in the kitchen of In De Wulf in Dranouter where he learned to create sublime dishes using the simplest local ingredients. He cooks with meat from small West Flanders farms, vegetables grown in the region and the freshest fish from the North Sea.

2 **DECOUVERTE**
Rijselsestraat 43
Ypres
Flanders Fields
+32 (0)57 48 92 48
*www.decouverte-
ieper.be*

This restaurant is run by a young couple in an elegant town house with wood floors and high ceilings. They aim to offer sophisticated cooking in a luxurious setting. Most of the time they succeed, although sometimes the food is slow to arrive. But we think this is a place to watch.

3 TRATTORIA ALLORO

Patersstraat 2
Ypres
Flanders Fields
+32 (0)57 36 53 75
www.trattoriaalloro.be

Here is a convivial Italian restaurant in a quiet side street a few minutes from the main square. You are welcomed by Fanny, who takes care of everything you need, while her British husband Patrick works in the kitchen creating hearty pasta dishes, hamburgers and steaks. Everything is cooked to perfection.

4 DEN OLIFANT

Diksmuidestraat 44
Ypres
Flanders Fields
+32 (0)57 36 73 62
www.den-olifant.be

Ruben and Margo run this lively restaurant in the town centre. The interior is decorated in a relaxed, modern style with white chairs and small round tables. The daily menu is chalked up on a blackboard. You can count on being served good Flemish cooking based on fish and meat, along with inspiring vegetarian dishes.

5 DE FONDERIE

Polenlaan 3
Ypres
Flanders Fields
+32 (0)57 36 45 80
defonderie.be

This is a stylish restaurant with a sober industrial interior located in an old factory. It is run by a young couple who set out to create the atmosphere of a 19th century Parisian brasserie. The cooking is based on Flemish and French recipes using fresh local ingredients.

The 5 most
ROMANTIC
RESTAURANTS *in Ypres*

6 **DE RUYFFELAER**
Gustave
De Stuersstraat 9
Ypres
Flanders Fields
+32 (0)57 36 60 06
www.deruyffelaer.be

This used to be the Café de la Tour (the old name can still be seen above No. 11). It is now an intimate Flemish restaurant decorated with wood panelling, antique clocks and old tools. An open fire is lit in winter to add to the romantic mood. The kitchen produces typical regional cooking such as wild boar pâté and rabbit simmered in beer with bacon and raisins, while beers include the house ale Oud Yper de Ruyffelaer.

7 **DE VOERMAN**
Rijselseweg 10
Ypres
Flanders Fields
+32 (0)479 50 58 49
www.devoerman.com

Nathalie Huys and her husband Christiaan have created a warm, romantic restaurant in restored stables that once belonged to a 19th century inn. Located just outside the town walls, De Voerman is a friendly place where you can eat tasty steaks cooked on an open grill, along with perfect frites. The terrace is an appealing spot on a summer evening.

8 CAPELLA

Kiekenmarkt 7
Ypres
Flanders Fields
+32 (0)57 36 61 32
*www.restaurant
capella.be*

This is an elegant restaurant with friendly young staff next to the old fish market in Ypres. The kitchen produces simple Belgian dishes, such as grilled Irish rib eye steak with frites, fried Ostend sole, and some appealing desserts.

9 DE STEENEN HAENE

Komenseweg 21
Ypres
Flanders Fields
+32 (0)57 20 54 86
www.desteenenhaene.be

This friendly Flemish restaurant is decorated in a warm rustic style with bare brick walls, old oak beams and a fire that is lit in winter. The kitchen produces a classic French style of cooking. De Steenen Haene lies a few kilometres out of town in an area dotted with war relics. The terrace at the back looks out on Zillebeke lake.

10 PACIFIC EILAND

Eiland 2
Ypres
Flanders Fields
+32 (0)57 20 05 28
pacificeiland.be

A little iron bridge takes you across the old moat to this romantic restaurant just beyond the city walls. It stands on an artificial island built in the 17th century under Spanish rule as part of the city's defences. The kitchen offers serious Flemish cooking including dishes made with fresh sole from the North Sea. You can also eat a simple lunch in the bistro, or sitting out on the terrace next to the water. Children like this place because of the indoor playground and the blue rowing boats you can hire.

10 PACIFIC EILAND

11 IN DE WULF

The 5 best places to eat in
FLANDERS FIELDS

---

11 **IN DE WULF**
Wulvestraat 1
Dranouter
Flanders Fields
+32 (0)57 44 55 67
indewulf.be

Kobe Desramaults has created a sublime restaurant in an authentic old Flemish farmhouse out in the misty fields. His young team produces astonishing meals composed of endless little dishes featuring excellent meat and fish, along with unusual vegetables supplied by local farms. His menus are not cheap, but then this has been ranked as one of the 100 best restaurants in the world. It also has rooms where you can stay the night.

12 **HOMMELHOF**
Watouplein 17
Watou
Flanders Fields
+32 (0)57 38 80 24
www.hommelhof.be

This is an attractive whitewashed country inn facing the village church in Watou. It is popular with local families as well as beer drinkers. The chef Stefaan Couttenye promotes the regional cooking of the Westhoek by digging up old recipes and using forgotten vegetables. Considered the godfather of Belgian beer cooking, he offers a range of dishes cooked with local beers like Watou Witbier and Sint-Bernardus Tripel. Seven local beers are available on tap including the lovely Hommelbier.

13 TERMINUS

Callicanneweg 16
Watou
Flanders Fields
+32 (0)57 38 80 87
*www.restaurant
terminus.be*

This friendly Flemish restaurant is run by the Verheyde family at an old border crossing. They offer honest Flemish cooking using the best ingredients, including beef from their own cattle. The wines are served by Pieter Verheyde, once voted best wine waiter in Belgium, who gave up his job in a three-star restaurant to return to his parents' place in the country.

14 HET OVENHUIS

Watouplein 1
Watou
Flanders Fields
+32 (0)57 38 83 38
www.hetovenhuis.be

This is a friendly family-run restaurant located in an old bakery on the main square in Watou, with old photographs on the walls and hop plants hanging from the ceiling. The menu includes local favourites like *garnaalkroketten*, along with some of the delicious Sint-Bernardus beers brewed in this region.

15 IN DE ZON

Dikkebusstraat 80
De Klijte
Flanders Fields
+32 (0)57 21 26 26
www.indezon.be

This is a charming Flemish country inn filled with antiques, old photographs and cycling memorabilia. It stands on a hill with a terrace that looks out across the rolling hills of Heuvelland. The owner Dirk is a former Belgian cyclist who has created a very convivial place to enjoy traditional Flemish food accompanied by a local beer.

The 5 best
POPERINGE AND
DIKSMUIDE *restaurants*

---

16 CAFÉ DE LA PAIX
Grote Markt 20
Poperinge
Flanders Fields
+32 (0)57 33 95 78
www.hoteldelapaix.be

This stylish restaurant belongs to a small family-run hotel on the main square in Poperinge. It is a friendly place with a skilled chef who prepares steaks in various ways as well as cooking with fish. The kitchen also does simple lunchtime cooking including the curious Poperinge speciality *Hennepot*.

17 PEGASUS
Guido Gezellestraat 7
Poperinge
Flanders Fields
+32 (0)57 33 57 25
www.pegasusrecour.be

This is a romantic restaurant located inside a beautiful old family-run hotel. The experienced chef Bert Recour prepares the food with great care using the best local ingredients, including hop shoots when they are in season. The terrace in the back garden is a lovely spot on a summer evening.

18 NOTARISHUYS
Koning
Albertstraat 39
Diksmuide
Flanders Fields
+32 (0)51 50 03 35
www.notarishuys.be

This is a stylish hotel restaurant located in a handsome old house on the edge of town that once belonged to the local notary. The chef creates interesting set menus using local vegetables and fresh fish.

19 'T SPARHOF

Stoppelweg 39
Poperinge
Flanders Fields
+32 (0)57 33 41 39
www.sparhof.be

This country inn lies a few kilometres out of Poperinge, not far from the Sint-Bernardus brewery. The interior is decorated in a rustic farmhouse style with a tiled floor, antique furniture and a blazing log fire in winter. The chef cooks steaks with creamy sauces, creative seafood dishes and several regional specialities, including huge juicy hams done in 'grandmother's style'.

20 DE VREDE

Grote Markt 35
Diksmuide
Flanders Fields
+32 (0)51 50 00 38
www.hoteldevrede.be

Here is a handsome old-fashioned hotel restaurant on the main square in Diksmuide. The kitchen produces good Flemish cooking including Ostend sole served with frites. The beer list includes exceptional Westvleteren beers brewed near here by Trappist monks.

The 5 most appealing
COUNTRY INNS
in French Flanders

---

21 **HAUT BONHEUR DE LA TABLE**

18 Grand-Place
Cassel
French Flanders
+33 (0)3 28 40 51 03
*www.hautbonheur
delatable.com*

This is a beautiful restaurant in an 18th century town house on the main square in Cassel. It has a grand interior with wood panelling and spectacular views from the terrace across the flat plains of Flanders. The chef offers innovative contemporary cooking including some spectacular desserts.

22 **AUBERGE DU VERT MONT**

1318 Rue du Mont Noir
Boeschepe
French Flanders
+33 (0)3 28 49 41 26
aubergeduvertmont.fr

This is a family-run country inn with exposed brick walls, an old wood-burning stove and sweeping views of the low hills around. The young chef had made his mark here by developing a creative cuisine using local ingredients and adding unexpected touches like frites served in a paper cone.

23 **AUBERGE DE LA BRIQUE D'OR**

Ancien Chemin de Bergues
Bourbourg
French Flanders
+33 (0)3 28 65 02 84

This is a friendly rustic inn attached to a farm. You are served hearty northern French cooking along with some good French wines. Children can run around the farmyard outside when they get bored.

24 HET BLAUWERSHOF

9 Rue d'Eecke
Godewaersvelde
French Flanders
+33 (0)3 28 49 45 11
www.estaminet-
blauwershof.com

The village of Godewaersvelde has a cluster of estaminets with old Flemish interiors. Het Blauwershof is one of the most authentic. It occupies an old forge with a tiled floor, battered furniture and a big iron stove. The kitchen produces Flemish-style food including chicken cooked in beer and the unavoidable *Potje Vleesch*. You can play old Flemish café games here, if you can understand the baffling rules.

25 AU PALAIS DU PICON

203 Rue Albert I
Bray-Dunes
French Flanders
+33 (0)3 28 26 54 40

This authentic dance café near the Belgian resort of De Panne offers a taste of old France. It is furnished in a nostalgic style with an ancient juke box and a disco ball. Locals come here to eat rabbit stew or drink a glass of *picon* (a local aperitif made using a secret recipe).

The 5 best places for
CREATIVE COOKING
at the coast

---

26 PHILIPPE NUYENS
J. De Troozlaan 78
Blankenberge
Belgian Coast
+32 (0)50 41 36 32

Philippe Nuyens runs a small restaurant on a busy avenue in Blankenberge. It is a comfortable, modest place with wood panelling and oak beams. It may not look like much, but the cooking is very good. Nuyens and his team keep things simple, using fish and shrimps fresh from the quayside, along with some less common fish. He sometimes borrows ideas from European regional cooking and adds unexpected touches like Poperinge hop shoots.

27 SEL GRIS
Zeedijk 314
Duinbergen
Belgian Coast
+32 (0)50 51 49 37
*www.restaurant
selgris.be*

This is a sober modern restaurant with views from the windows of the stormy grey sea. It is located in the quiet seaside resort of Duinbergen, a few kilometres down the coast from flashy Knokke. The cooking is done by the young Flemish chef Frederik Deceuninck, who reinvents old Belgian recipes to create stunning dishes full of subtle flavours.

28 MARKT XI

Driftweg 11
De Haan
Belgian Coast
+32 (0)59 43 44 44
www.markt11.be

Benny Van Torre is a young Flemish chef who runs a cool, contemporary restaurant in an old De Haan seaside house decorated with white walls and designer lamps. Van Torre grew up in a fishing family and claims to know where to get the best sole in the world. Having trained as a butcher, he also knows how to get his hands on the most succulent Belgian pork. He works in an open kitchen creating some of the most adventurous food on the coast.

29 BISTRO MATHILDA

Leopold II-laan 1
Ostend
Belgian Coast
+32 (0)59 51 06 70
www.bistromathilda.be

This modern Belgian brasserie facing the park gets its name from the female sculpture opposite known locally as *Dikke Mathilda* (Fat Mathilda). It is a crowded, lively place offering traditional Belgian dishes like shrimp croquettes and mussels, but also local specialities such as *tatjespap met Oostendse grijze garnalen en gepocheerd hoeve-eitje* (mashed potatoes served with grey Ostend shrimps and poached farmhouse egg).

30 GRAND CABARET

Kaai 12
Nieuwpoort
Belgian Coast
+32 (0)493 72 96 51
grandcabaret.be

Vincent Florizoone runs a trendy restaurant on the quayside in Nieuwpoort that feels more like a sexy Parisian night club. He has developed a very personal style over the years which he likes to call kinky cooking. It is a fun, friendly place to come if you are willing to try out offbeat cooking by one of the country's most inventive chefs.

The 5 best places for
FRESH FISH FROM THE NORTH SEA

---

31 SAVARIN
Albert I-
promenade 75
Ostend
Belgian Coast
+32 (0)59 51 31 71
www.savarin.be

This is a smart restaurant for a special meal at the coast. Everything is perfect, from the starched white table cloths to the glorious views of the sea. The kitchen is run by the young chef Floris Panckoucke who cooks exceptional dishes featuring the freshest fish. His training is classical, but he brings a creative edge to everything he puts on the plate.

32 CAFÉ DE PARIS
Kaai 16
Nieuwpoort
Belgian Coast
+32 (0)58 24 04 80
www.cafedeparis.be

A traditional French-style brasserie near the port with small tables inside and a terrace for summer days. Here you can eat North Sea sole freshly landed a few hours earlier, tasty shrimps scooped from the shallows off the coast or oysters from Brittany. It's not a cheap place to eat, but it is somewhere special.

33 FLAVIE'S TAFEL
Langestraat 115
Nieuwpoort
Belgian Coast
+32 (0)58 23 73 86
www.flaviestafel.be

Flavie's Tafel used to stand on the harbour front, but moved recently to a nearby street away from the port. It now has a severe modern interior, but the kitchen still produces the same refined fish cooking.

34 CROMWELL

Wapenplein 6
Ostend
Belgian Coast
+32 (0)59 70 06 05

This is an old style Belgian fish restaurant on the main square in Ostend with a relaxed atmosphere. Locals come here for the fresh oysters, crisply-fried shrimp croquettes and plump Ostend sole. It's possibly a bit crowded, but it has an appealing Belgian atmosphere and some very friendly waiters who never let a wine glass stand empty for long.

35 MARTINS VISRESTAURANT

Sint-Donaaskerk-
straat 19
Zeebrugge
Belgian Coast
+32 (0)50 54 43 27
*www.martins
visrestaurant.be*

This restaurant is located next to a tram stop near Zeebrugge harbour. The interior is decorated in a cool maritime style with white tablecloths and little model ships. Wendy welcomes you at the door while her husband Christophe cooks the food. Together they have created one of the best fish restaurants on the coast, where you can eat delicious fried sole and Norwegian Arctic cod.

The 5 best restaurants for
A STEAMING POT
OF MUSSELS

---

36 DE MOSSELBEURS
Dwarsstraat 10
Ostend
Belgian Coast
+32 (0)59 80 73 10

Here is one of the best places on the coast to eat mussels. It is a striking, contemporary restaurant with a black-and-white tiled floor, lamps hung from wooden winches and a spiral staircase leading to a romantic mezzanine. It all feels very shipshape. The diners sit in straight rows at tables covered with starched white cloths. The mussels come in traditional black pots, swimming in a sea of chopped vegetables.

37 OESTERPUT
Wenduinse
Steenweg 16
Blankenberge
Belgian Coast
+32 (0)50 41 10 35
oesterput.com

No booking. Nothing fancy. Just perfect seafood. The Devriendt family runs a huge wooden restaurant on the quayside that looks like a New England clam shack. It is very basic, but they serve some of the best seafood on the coast, including dripping wet oysters, little whelks that have to be extracted from their shell with a pin and freshly-cooked lobsters that are kept in large tanks.

38 KOMBUIS

Van Iseghemlaan 24
Ostend
Belgian Coast
+32 (0)59 80 16 49

Kombuis is not much more than a basic chip shop with an unpretentious 1960s interior and tables covered with white paper. But it is one of the best places in Belgium to eat mussels. The place is run by a friendly mother and son team who serve up big white bowls overflowing with steamy mussels buried under a mound of celery. It's terribly small, but Belgians are happy to squeeze inside to enjoy the friendly, nostalgic atmosphere. Booking is a must.

39 DE MARKT

Marktplein 10
Nieuwpoort
Belgian Coast
+32 (0)486 26 33 99
www.demarkt
nieuwpoort.be

This is a bustling place to eat overlooking the main square in Nieuwpoort. The staff are friendly and the cooking is well done. Many Belgians come here to eat a traditional pot of mussels served with frites, but you can also order a simple steak or sole.

40 RESTO REAL

Koninklijke Baan 198
Koksijde
Belgian Coast
+32 (0)58 51 28 02
www.restoreal.be

This is a bustling family restaurant that has been serving mussels along with other classic Belgian dishes since 1980. The interior is rather austere, but the mussels are perfectly done. The staff are friendly, although the food is sometimes slow to arrive at busy times.

36 DE MOSSELBEURS

37 OESTERPUT

44 FORT NAPOLEON

The 5
COOLEST PLACES
TO EAT *at the coast*

---

41 **LE COUP VERT**
   Sparrendreef 92
   Het Zoute
   Belgian Coast
   +32 (0)50 62 70 14
   www.knokke.
   lecoupvert.com

Christian Souvereyns is a creative Belgian chef who runs a tiny delicatessen hidden away in a quiet street in Het Zoute. It has a bar at the front where you can eat a simple lunch and an attractive little room at the back. You have to book, but it is worth it because Souvereyns' Mediterranean-style cooking is exceptional.

42 **CICCIO**
   Dumortierlaan 64
   Knokke
   Belgian Coast
   +32 (0)50 60 96 61
   www.ciccio.be

Claudio Dell'Anno took over from his father to run this little Italian restaurant in Knokke. The interior is decorated in a severe modern style with black walls and bare wood tables. But the staff who work here are not at all forbidding. The chef won a TV talent contest in 2009 so the Italian-style cooking is absolutely stunning. But it is not cheap.

43 BRASSERIE OOSTERSTAKETSEL

Oosterstaketsel
Blankenberge
Belgian Coast
+32 (0)476 66 49 98
www.oosterstaketsel.be

You can walk out on the wooden jetty at Blankenberge built in 1860 to reach a stylish white cabin perched above the waves. This is a wonderful spot to sit in winter with a dark Trappist beer. Or you can soak up the sun on the outdoor terrace in the summer.

44 FORT NAPOLEON

Vuurtorenweg
Ostend
Belgian Coast
+32 (0)59 32 00 48
www.fort-napoleon.be

A striking contemporary restaurant has been created inside the massive brick walls of an old Napoleonic fortress. The interior was designed by Fabiaan Van Severen, who comes from a family of Belgian designers. It is divided into a chic dining room where the food is serious French cuisine and a more informal bistro with a terrace nestling in the dunes. This is somewhere to come in the summer to eat shrimp croquettes or a salad.

45 CUINES 33

Smedenstraat 33
Knokke
Belgian Coast
+32 (0)50 60 60 69
www.cuines33.be

This is a trendy modern restaurant in a quiet street far from the crowded beach. It was designed by interior architect Lieven Musschoot in a laid-back lounge style with blue banquettes, cushions and dark tropical wood tables. The cooking is inspired by the fashionable Barcelona scene, which means inventive little tapas dishes brought to the table by the chef. But little dishes don't mean little prices, at least not in Knokke.

The 5 best places for
SERIOUS STEAKS AND BURGERS

---

46 DEN ARTIEST
Kapucijnenstraat 13
Ostend
Belgian Coast
+32 (0)59 80 88 89
www.artiest.be

This restaurant is located in a stunning 1902 building on two floors that once belonged to a glassworks. The interior is decorated in a flamboyant style with big mirrors and wood panelling. This is a place to eat huge racks of grilled ribs served with herb butter. It's a noisy, friendly, bustling place that is hard not to like, even if the food can take some time.

47 DE MIKKE
Leopold II Laan 82
Oostduinkerke
Belgian Coast
+32 (0)58 52 19 45
www.demikke.be

Located away from the beach in Oost-duinkerke village, this busy restaurant has been around since 1976. It's a simple, friendly place where they serve big steaks with frites on wooden boards. You can't book a table, but the waiters will try to squeeze you in somewhere.

48 BRASSERIE RUBENS

Zeedijk-
Albertstrand 589
Knokke
Belgian Coast
+32 (0)50 60 35 01
www.brasserie-rubens.be

This is a lively seafront brasserie with a large terrace. It is a friendly, efficient place where you get classic Belgian food like shrimp croquettes and steaks served with creamy pepper sauce.

49 BISTRO DE TIJD

Grote Markt 9
Blankenberge
Belgian Coast
+32 (0)473 75 43 56
www.bistro-detijd.be

This is a sober modern bistro on the main square in Blankenberge where the kitchen prepares classic Belgian dishes like shrimp croquettes, Ostend sole and Irish rib eye steaks. The staff are friendly and take care of every detail.

50 COOK & ROLL

Kursaal-Oosthelling 4
Ostend
+32 (0)486 73 88 83
www.cookandroll.be

Here is a relaxed new place near the casino for a serious burger and frites. The owner cooks the homemade burgers in an open kitchen while rock music plays in the background. He has some excellent beers in stock including some from small West Flanders breweries like De Struise Brouwers and De Ranke. This place has a cool, laid-back mood that suits Ostend.

The 5 best places to eat
SHRIMP CROQUETTES

---

51 **BRASSERIE BRISTOL**
Zeedijk 291
Knokke
Belgian Coast
+32 (0)50 51 21 12
brasseriebristol.be

This is a striking brasserie in a modern building on the Heist seafront. It stands on the site of the old Bristol Hotel built in 1927. The brasserie opened in 2008 with a menu offering those simple, classic dishes that Belgians like to eat at the coast, such as tomatoes filled with grey shrimps, croquettes and Ostend sole. It is worth asking for a table by the window to enjoy the stunning view.

52 **BISTRO MERLOT**
Nieuwpoortlaan 70B
De Panne
Belgian Coast
+32 (0)58 41 40 61

This is an elegant restaurant with a warm, bustling interior. It is decorated with mirrors, soft lights and photographs of French film stars, which makes it feel more like Paris than De Panne. This is somewhere to come to taste fresh homemade shrimp croquettes along with chunky golden hand-cut frites. You also get very good steaks here.

53 LA GALLERIA

James Ensor-
galerij 30-32
Ostend
Belgian Coast
+32 (0)59 70 01 50
*www.lagalleria
oostende.be*

This is a tiny place hidden away in a 19th century arcade. It is worth coming here to taste the *garnaalkroketten*, deep-fried croquettes filled with tiny pink North Sea shrimps. They are served with a generous topping of deep-fried parsley and a slice of lemon. You can also eat a plate of Ostend oysters when they are in season, or a whole lobster. But there are only a few tables, so you need to book.

54 'T WERFTJE

Werfkaai
Zeebrugge
Belgian Coast

Mike and Herlinde run an old café on the harbour front in Zeebrugge that has been around for more than a century. It's a plain, friendly place with wood panelling and mirrors, where fishermen drop by for a bowl of fish soup or Herlinde's famous *garnaalkroketten*.

55 PLASSENDALE

Oudenburgse-
steenweg 123
Ostend
Belgian Coast
+32 (0)59 26 70 35
*www.restaurant-
plassendale.be*

This is an appealing family-run restaurant outside Ostend on the banks of the canal that runs to Bruges. The chef cooks classic Belgian brasserie dishes including a delicious bouillabaisse and tasty shrimp croquettes served with deep-fried parsley. The waterfront terrace is a good spot to eat in the summer, but you will have to book.

The 5 best places for
CHEAP EATS

---

56 DE PEERDEVISSCHER
Pastoor
Schmitzstraat 4
Oostduinkerke
Belgian Coast
+32 (0)58 51 32 57

This simple whitewashed Flemish tavern next to the Fishing Museum serves some of the best seafood on the coast. The interior has an appealing rustic look with red-and-white checked tablecloths and old nautical mementoes. The kitchen produces plates of little sole fried in butter accompanied by bowls of golden frites. The owner is an authentic shrimp fisherman who rides on horseback into the waves to gather the little grey shrimps.

57 TAVERNE KOEKOEK
Langestraat 38
Ostend
Belgian Coast
+32 (0)59 70 89 70

This is somewhere to come if you have a craving for roast chicken. The interior is decorated in a plain style that dates back to the 1970s. You sit at long wooden tables under strange ceiling frescos. It's very basic. But the chicken cooked on a spit is delicious. It comes on a plate with a basket of sliced bread and a beer. Nothing more. You have to eat the chicken with your hands and tidy up afterwards with a moist wipe.

58 RENÉ'S IN DE STAD KORTRIJK

Langestraat 119
Ostend
Belgian Coast
+32 (0)59 70 71 89

René Coolsaet runs a simple fish restaurant named after the Belgian town where his father was born. He cooks the food himself in a tiny basement kitchen and brings it to the table all on his own. The Ostend sole comes with homemade chips and a pot of mayonnaise. Nowhere does it cheaper. Or better.

59 'T WATERHUIS

Vindictivelaan 35
Ostend
Belgian Coast
+32 (0)59 80 32 73
www.twaterhuis.be

This bustling brasserie stands on the harbour in Ostend. It occupies an old inn dating back to 1623 where seamen used to come to buy drinking water. The kitchen produces simple food like homemade shrimp croquettes or spaghetti vongole. But you can also come here for coffee and apple cake, or a pancake in the afternoon.

60 CHARLIE'S LUNCHROOM

Albert I laan 326
Nieuwpoort
Belgian Coast
www.charlies lunchroom.be

Here is a cool spot in Nieuwpoort for a quick lunch. The interior architect Lieven Musschoot has created a relaxed bistro interior with a black counter, recycled wallpaper and solid armchairs. The chef offers a limited menu that includes tapas dishes, lasagna and hamburgers. You can also drop in for a coffee in the afternoon, or a gin and tonic after the beach.

The 5 best shops for
BELGIAN CHOCOLATES

---

61 CHOCOLATIER M
Sylvain
Dupuisstraat 38
Knokke
Belgian Coast
+32 (0)50 61 44 60
www.chocolatier-m.be

David Maenhout started making chocolate in chic Knokke in 2005. He creates tiny chocolates in a workshop behind his shop using the finest Belgian chocolate. He comes up with endless ideas for combining different flavours like mango with balsamic vinegar, or lemon with coriander seeds. But not just any lemon. It has to be calamansi lemon from South East Asia.

62 CHOCOLATERIE LEDOUX
Boezingestraat 133
Langemark
Flanders Fields
+32 (0)57 48 92 22
www.choc-ledoux.be

This chocolate shop is not that easy to find. It is located in a modern house out in the countryside on the road from Ypres to Langemark. Founded in the 1970s, it is now run by a young couple who make authentic chocolates in a workshop next to the shop. They specialise in seashells which they make by hand in special moulds. You can call in to watch them at work on Friday at 10.30 am and Saturday at 3 pm.

63 FREDERIC BLONDEEL

Zeelaan 333
Koksijde
Belgian Coast
+32 (0)58 51 09 40
*www.frederic
blondeel.com*

Frederic Blondeel makes chocolates in a workshop in the village of Beauvoorde, but sells them in a shop in the beach town of Koksijde. He uses the best cocoa beans from Africa to make classic Belgian chocolates.

64 DELHY

Kerkstraat 31
Blankenberge
Belgian Coast
+32 (0)50 41 74 96
www.chocolatesonline.be

This family-run shop behind the dike in Blankenberge has been selling Belgian chocolates since 1958. They make original chocolates with unusual and mysterious flavours using the purest cocoa butter. We love the occasional surprises like tiny raisins buried in the chocolates.

65 DE WITTE PAREL

Vijfhoekstraat 19
Watou
Flanders Fields
+32 (0)479 28 45 10

Gwendoline Desmit opened her chocolate shop in 2012 in a brick house off the main square in Watou. She sells delicious homemade chocolates in an old-fashioned interior, as well as bottles of the local Sint-Bernardus beers.

62 CHOCOLATERIE LEDOUX

The 5 best places for
ICE CREAM

---

66 **GLACIER DE LA POSTE**

**Zeedijk Het Zoute 718
Knokke
Belgian Coast
+32 (0)50 60 80 41**

This shiny modern ice cream salon has been around for more than 40 years. It used to be located next to a post office, but now occupies a corner building looking out to sea. They make a huge range of flavours including candy floss and pine nuts. You can perch on a stool inside the shop or sit out on a wooden deck overlooking the beach.

67 **'T ZOET GENOT**

**Zeedijk 476
Oostduinkerke
Belgian Coast
+32 (0)58 52 07 47
www.zoetgenot.be**

You can't go to the beach without eating an ice cream. Here is one place to try out. Located near the beach in Oost-duinkerke, it has a terrace where elderly Belgian couples sit out in the summer while their dog laps up water from a silver bowl. You can also pick up a cone at a side window or sit inside to eat a dame blanche.

68 IJS RENÉ

Leopoldlaan 22
De Haan
Belgian Coast
+32 (0)59 23 54 53
www.ijsrene.be

This simple ice cream salon has been around for more than 50 years. It is now run by a couple who make delicious ice cream using goats' milk supplied by an organic farm outside De Haan.

69 DE IJSHOEVE

Oude Damse Weg 2A
Vivenkapelle
Bruges Countryside
+32 (0)50 37 39 87
www.deijshoeve.be

You have to leave the coast behind to taste De IJshoeve ice cream. It is made on a farm near Damme using milk from dairy cows that graze in the nearby meadows. The farm shop sells about 15 different flavours including some rather exotic tastes. Kids love to come here because it has a playground.

70 AU PINGOUIN

Kerkstraat 33
Blankenberge
Belgian Coast
+32 (0)50 41 27 85

This is a traditional ice cream salon just behind the sea dike in Blankenberge. They make the ice cream in shiny machines behind the counter and bring it to the table in chilled silver bowls. It is friendly and correct, but the interior is a bit charmless.

The 5 best
FISH MARKETS AND FISHMONGERS

---

71 **VISTRAP**
Visserskaai
Ostend
Belgian Coast

The quayside fish market in Ostend is a lively, friendly place where locals go to buy fresh sole and North Sea shrimps brought to shore just a few hours earlier. Many of the stands are run by fishermen's wives who remain cheerful even in a howling gale. We tend to stop at the stand called Lima which is run by an Ostend fishing family.

72 **WESTHINDER**
Vismijnstraat 20
Zeebrugge
Belgian Coast
+32 (0)50 54 41 47

This is an outstanding fishmongers located opposite the old fish market in Zeebrugge. It is run by a friendly couple who visit the new fish market on the other side of the harbour to pick up fresh sole, skate and plaice, along with little shrimps, cockles and whelks.

73 **JENS VISHANDEL**
Kaai 37
Nieuwpoort
Belgian Coast
+32 (0)58 23 42 57
www.jensnv.be

Jens Vishandel is one of the best fishmongers on the quayside in Nieuwpoort. The owner buys North Sea fish fresh every day in Nieuwpoort and Zeebrugge, along with the best Zeeland mussels.

74 AU SAUMON D'OR

Zeelaan 261
Koksijde
Belgian Coast
+32 (0)58 52 40 92
www.deklipper.be

This is one of the best fishmongers on the coast, where several famous chefs come to buy their fish. The owners buy North Sea fish fresh every day in Dunkirk and import more unusual varieties from Denmark and Iceland. The shop also sells delicious take away fish dishes.

75 VISHANDEL DE PAEPE

Knokkestraat 20
Knokke
Belgian Coast
+32 (0)50 51 13 16
www.vishandel depaepe.be

Locals have been coming to this shop to buy oysters and lobsters since 1928. It is still owned by the Depaepe family, who have built up a reputation for selling the freshest fish caught by Zeebrugge trawlers, along with lobster from the Scheldt and mussels cultivated in Zeeland.

NIEUWPOORT FISH MARKET

The 5
SPECIALITIES TO EAT
IN THE WESTHOEK

---

76 **MAZARINETAART**
BANKETBAKKERIJ SANSEN
Gasthuisstraat 36
Poperinge
Flanders Fields
+32 (0)57 33 31 90

This sweet sponge cake is a Poperinge speciality named after a Cardinal Jules Mazarin who invented the recipe in 1885. He took sponge cake and soaked it in warm butter and cinnamon sauce to create a sweet, sticky pudding. You can pick it up in a plastic box at Sansen's bakery on the main street. "We were already here in 1914," it says on a sign outside.

77 **BIERPATÉ**
PUYDTJES
Neermarkt 2
Ypres
Flanders Fields
+32 (0)57 20 05 33
www.puydtjes.be

This is a tasty speciality of the Westhoek that you can find in many local butchers. There are different recipes involving local beers, but a little shop in Ypres called Puydtjes is the only place where you can buy paté made with Sint-Bernardus Abt 12. This shop also sells a delicious Ypres paté made with Calvados as well as an old-style *boerenpaté* based on a recipe from 1907.

78 PASSENDALE CHEESE

DE OUDE KAASMAKERIJ
's Graventafel-
straat 48A
Passendale
Flanders Fields
+32 (0)51 77 70 05
*www.deoudekaas
makerij.be*

The battle of Passchendaele was fought on agricultural land where dairy cows now graze. They produce the milk used to make the delicious soft yellow Passendale cheese. You can watch it being made and taste the final product at De Oude Kaasmakerij out in the fields near Tyne Cot Cemetery.

79 VERWENKOFFIE

CASINO
Polenlaan 7
Kemmel
Flanders Fields
+32 (0)57 85 98 30
www.casinokemmel.be

Coffee in the Westhoek is often accompanied by a generous assortment of little nibbles on a tray, such as sponge cake, or a Belgian chocolate or even a small glass of alcohol. One of the best assortments is served at Casino in Kemmel, an Art Deco restaurant that once had a casino. Here the coffee comes on a tray with cake, a biscuit, a gummy bear and a small glass of *advocaat*.

80 POTJEVLEESCH

'T PATÉWINKELTJE /
DE VEURN' AMBACHTSE
Kaatsspelstraat 5
Alveringem
French Flanders
+32 (0)58 29 89 33
*www.deveurn
ambachtse.be*

You often find this strange dish on the menu in small inns close to the French border. Originally a mediaeval dish eaten in the Dunkirk region, the name means a "little pot of meat". The recipe can vary, but it is normally made with chicken, rabbit and veal preserved in jelly. Local people love it, served with a bowl of frites and a beer.

The 5
SPECIALITIES OF THE BELGIAN COAST

---

81 **SHRIMP CROQUETTES**

Belgians love to eat *garnaalkroketten* when they are at the coast. These tasty little croquettes are served in grand old restaurants with white linen on the tables as well as simple beach bars in the dunes. They are made with the tiny grey North Sea shrimps that are fished from the North Sea shallows every morning. These are stirred into a béchamel sauce, deep fried and served with a sprig of deep-fried parsley.

82 **MUSSELS**

The coast is lined with family restaurants where you can eat big black pots filled with steaming mussels cooked in a vegetable broth of chopped onions, celery and white wine. Most of the mussels come from the Dutch province of Zeeland where the conditions are perfect for breeding the small barnacle-encrusted black shellfish.

83 BABELUTTEN

Kerkstraat 70
Blankenberge
Belgian Coast
+32 (0)50 41 21 72
www.moederbabelutte.com

You will see the old Moeder Babelutte sweet shops in several resorts along the coast. They are easy to spot with their blue and white striped awnings and old-fashioned interiors. They sell traditional hard sweets wrapped in waxed paper, which were originally made by fishermen's wives using butter from polder farms.

84 KEYTE

A group of beer enthusiasts called the Oostendse Bierjutters launched a new beer called Keyte in 2004 to mark the anniversary of the Siege of Ostend. Brewed by the Strubbe brewery, Keyte Triple is now sold in many local cafés.

85 WAFFLES

Everyone in Belgium dreams of eating the perfect waffle at the seaside. It has to be a gaufre de Bruxelles, plump and crisp, served on a white plate with a dusting of icing sugar.

KAFFEE BAZAAR

50 PLACES
FOR A DRINK

The 5 best **TRADITIONAL BARS** in Ypres —— 52

The 5 best **TRADITIONAL CAFES**
in Flanders Fields ———————————— 54

The 5 best **COFFEE HOUSES** in Ypres ———— 56

The 5 best **CAFÉS IN POPERINGE** ———————— 58

The 5 best places to play **TRADITIONAL
CAFÉ GAMES** ———————————— 60

The 5 best places for a **COFFEE
AT THE COAST** ———————————— 62

The 5 best places to **DRINK
A BELGIAN BEER** in Ostend ————— 64

The 5 best **BEACH BARS** ————————— 66

The 5 coolest spots for **COCKTAILS** at the coast — 68

The 5 best **LOCAL BEERS**
from independent breweries ———————— 70

The 5 best
TRADITIONAL BARS
in Ypres

---

86 **DE 12 APOSTELS**
   D'Hondtstraat 18
   Ypres
   Flanders Fields

Christophe Gantois opened the coolest bar in Ypres in 2000. It is a relaxed spot with a dark red interior filled with religious statues, paintings of Jesus and faded LP covers. The beer list is not long, but it includes some fine local bottled beers like Sint-Bernardus 12 and Omer. It attracts a friendly mix of young musicians, teenagers drinking mojitos and tourists who have strayed from the main square.

87 **THE TIMES**
   Korte Torhoutstraat 7
   Ypres
   Flanders Fields
   +32 (0)473 66 45 81
   www.the-times-ypres.be

This bar is hidden down a side street just off the main square. Look for the Union Jack flag and you have found it. It appears rather sober from the street, but the interior is warm with a long marble bar, wood panelling and old Ypres posters on the walls. The owner Alain is serious about beer and keeps Sint-Bernardus Wit on tap along with the local Ypres pils. He also has a good selection of excellent beers by small local breweries such as Van Eecke and De Dolle Brouwers.

88 KAFFEE BAZAAR

Boomgaardstraat 9
Ypres
Flanders Fields
+32 (0)494 53 32 50
www.kaffeebazaar.be

This convivial café moved in 2014 to a new location. The interior already looks old with wood tables, framed fashion prints and long candles on the tables. The café stocks about 100 beers including some that you don't find in many bars, like De Ranke XXX Bitter and La Trappe Quadrupel Oak Aged.

89 'T KLEIN RIJSEL

Rijselstraat 208
Ypres
Flanders Fields
+32 (0)57 20 02 36

This is a warm, atmospheric bar next to the Lille Gate heated by an old gas fire in winter. It is decorated with an odd collection of paintings, old weapons and dusty war relics. The bar stocks about 40 different beers and includes some from small family breweries, and a house beer called Vredesbier served in heavy stone jugs.

90 THE FAT CAT

D'Hondtstraat 9
Ypres
Flanders Fields
+32 (0)489 80 12 71

The owner of the 12 Apostels opened this bar in the same street in 2013. Groups of young people come here to perch on high stools at round tables, trying to hold a conversation while old school hard rock blasts out from the speakers. The table football machine just adds to the noise level. The drink list chalked on a long blackboard includes some interesting local brews like Adriaen Brouwer and Hommelbier.

The 5 best
TRADITIONAL CAFÉS
in Flanders Fields

---

91 SAINT-HUBERT

Sint-Medardus-
plein 17
Wijtschate
Flanders Fields
+32 (0)476 46 44 23
*www.sainthubert
wijtschate.be*

Peter and Cindy run a bustling café on Wijtschate village square where locals mix with ramblers and war tourists. The interior is decorated with rustic pine walls, bare wooden tables and odd relics of the war. The beer list includes Brugse Zot on tap and the local Hommelbier. Cindy cooks simple tavern food including steaks, ribs and omelettes.

92 IN DE VREDE

Donkerstraat 13
Westvleteren
Flanders Fields
+32 (0)57 40 03 77
www.indevrede.be

Beer drinkers love this café, although it is hardly beautiful. It is located in a modern brick building owned by the Sint-Sixtus abbey. Beer lovers come here from all over the world to drink the very rare and coveted Westvleteren 12 beer brewed by the Trappist monks across the road. You can order bread and cheese to eat, but not much more. The abbey shop sometimes sells Westvleteren beers to take away. And sometimes it doesn't.

93 DE BARBIER

Hillestraat 5
Dranouter
Flanders Fields

This is a traditional Flemish café out in the countryside near the French border. Decorated with old wood panelling, shiny parquet and a set of old scales, it's a friendly local place to stop for a beer or a simple lunch. You can ask for shrimp croquettes or the local speciality *potjevleesch* if you are feeling adventurous.

94 DEN EKSTER

Lettingstraat 42
Dranouter
Flanders Fields
+32 (0)57 44 68 52
www.den-ekster.com

This lively music café occupies a restored farmhouse out in the countryside. It regularly stages folk concerts in an old barn, and attracts a young friendly crowd. The kitchen offers everything from a simple sandwich to grilled ribs, while the bar has six beers on tap including Hommelbier.

95 DE TERE PLEKKE

Koudekotsstraat 21
Dranouter
Flanders Fields
+32 (0)57 44 65 67
www.detereplekke.fr

Here is a rustic inn out in the Flemish countryside near the French border with an ancient stove in the middle of the room and hops hanging down from the roof. The food is quite plain, but the list of beers contains some fine ales from small Belgian breweries.

The 5 best
COFFEE HOUSES
in Ypres

---

96 **'T BINNENHUYS**
Gustave De Stuers-
straat 8
Ypres
Flanders Fields
+32 (0)57 35 97 06

You find a secret romantic café hidden at the back of a rambling mansion dating from 1772. Located in an interior design shop, the café takes up two small rooms furnished with old leather sofas, antique lamps and faded photographs. You can come here in the afternoon for coffee and cake sitting next to the old iron stove.

97 **GOSSIP**
Vandenpeereboom-
plein 29
Ypres
Flanders Fields
+32 (0)57 36 08 45

This is a modern coffee bar with bright orange chairs and a terrace overlooking the St. Martin's Cathedral. The owner makes good espresso coffee with Illy beans along with waffles, pancakes and sandwiches.

98 **ALLEGRIA**
Vandenpeereboom-
plein 3
Ypres
+32 (0)57 42 22 28
www.allegriafoodbar.be

Allegria is a friendly lunchroom in a reconstructed Flemish gable house near the cloth hall. The interior is furnished in a modern style with a long list of sandwiches chalked on the blackboard. You can come here for breakfast or sit with a coffee on the pavement terrace.

99 KARAMEL

Menenstraat 9
Ypres
Flanders Fields

This is an appealing little coffee shop on the street leading to the Menin Gate. They make good espresso coffee, along with delicious hot chocolate. You can buy tea and coffee in the small shop, along with coffee-making accessories, tea pots and local beers.

100 MIMI'S

Boterstraat 45
Ypres
Flanders Fields
+32 (0)57 36 65 68
www.mimi-s.be

This is a romantic coffee house decorated with old lamps, mirrors and leather sofas. Retro jazz plays softly in the background. It feels as if you have stumbled into an eccentric uncle's living room. The friendly young owners Dries and Julia make excellent coffee and sublime hot chocolate. But they are open at odd times.

96 'T BINNENHUYS

The 5 best
CAFÉS IN POPERINGE

---

101 LA POUPÉE
Grote Markt 16
Poperinge
Flanders Fields
+32 (0)57 33 30 08

This old-fashioned tea room on the main square in Poperinge takes its name from a famous café that was reserved for officers during the First World War. The interior is decorated in a quaint style with floral wallpaper, chandeliers and 18th century military portraits.

102 DE STADSSCHAAL
Gasthuisstraat 69
Poperinge
Flanders Fields

Here is a typical old Flemish bar with solid wooden furniture, curious paintings and hops hanging from the ceiling. But it isn't as authentic as it looks. It was once a family home where the Belgian astronaut Dirk Frimout was born. Now it is part of the Hop Museum.

103 OUD VLAENDEREN
Grote Markt 14
Poperinge
Flanders Fields
+32 (0)57 36 86 85

This traditional café was saved from demolition in 2011 by a local hop farmer. He has turned it into a specialised beer café promoting Belgian hop beers. The interior is furnished in old Flemish style while TV screens show live football matches and cycle races.

104 HET MYSTERIE

Abeelseweg 29
Poperinge
Flanders Fields
+32 (0)57 36 35 80

Here is a bizarre local café on the edge of Poperinge with a menacing witch standing next to the door. The interior is filled with strange objects including a black cauldron hanging from the ceiling. But do not panic. This is a friendly place with a good range of beers and a collection of traditional Flemish wooden pub games to play on a winter evening.

105 WALLY'S FARM

Abeelseweg 232
Poperinge
Flanders Fields
+32 (0)57 33 52 24
www.wallysfarm.be

Wally restored an old Flemish farmhouse outside Poperinge to create a rustic restaurant. The walls are covered with Elvis memorabilia collected by Wally over the years. He used to perform Elvis songs here every night. Now he says he is too old. But this is still a lively spot to come on an evening with a bunch of friends.

101 LA POUPÉE

102 DE STANDSSCHAAL

The 5 best places to play
TRADITIONAL CAFÉ GAMES

———————

106 BOERENHOL
Driegoenstraat 4
Reningelst
Flanders Fields
+32 (0)57 36 02 53
www.boerenhol.be

The Boerenhol is an attractive village café near Poperinge with a large terrace looking out on the fields and a long list of local West Flanders beers. To add to its charm, it has a collection of old wooden café games including an ancient French game called *Trou Madame*.

107 AU NOUVEAU ST-ELOI
Gemenestraat 4
Watou
Flanders Fields
+32 (0)494 13 68 30
www.aunouveau st-eloi.be

Here is an authentic Flemish village café not far from the French border where you can sit out on the terrace with a glass of Watou beer. Or you can go inside with the locals and try your hand at one of the old café games such as *sjoelbak*.

108 IN BEVEREN
Roesbruggestraat 20
Beveren aan de IJzer
Flanders Fields
+32 (0)57 30 05 73
www.inbeveren.be

This friendly tavern lies in a village near the French border. You can stop here for a local beer and a quick game of *hamertjesspel*, an old Flemish café game that goes back to at least 1750 in which players try to hit a small lead ball into the opposite goal using a little wooden mallet.

109 DE HELLEKETEL

Vuile Seulestraat 6
Watou
Flanders Fields
+32 (0)57 38 80 35

This old Flemish bar stands on a deserted country road near Watou. It is a dark, slightly creepy place (the name means Witches' cauldron) that has been here since 1895. The interior is decorated with a tiled floor and antique furniture. There are old café games to play, and some exceptional beers to drink.

110 HET JAGERSHOF

Bankelindeweg 58
Krombeke
Flanders Fields
+32 (0)57 33 55 25
www.hetjagershof.be

Here is an old Flemish café surrounded by woods where you can sometimes spot deer. The rustic interior is filled with old paintings, iron lamps and a collection of decorated biscuit tins. The owner has also created a private war museum based on diaries kept by the monks at Sint-Sixtus abbey. You can order a beer and go out the back to play *hoefijzerwerpen*, a game in which you throw horseshoes.

CAFÉ GAMES

The 5 best places for a
COFFEE AT
THE COAST

---

111 DU PARC
   Marie-Joséplein 3
   Ostend
   Belgian Coast
   +32 (0)59 51 13 05
   www.brasserieduparc.be

The hotel has hardly changed since it opened in the 1920s. Furnished with old leather sofas, brass coat hooks and large mirrors, it is staffed by formal waiters in black aprons who glide around bearing trays of drinks. The coffee is made using an old pewter canister filled with boiling water that slowly dribbles into the cup.

112 ANTIQUE CAFÉ
   Lippenslaan 135
   Knokke
   Belgian Coast
   +32 (0)50 62 50 50
   www.antiquecafe.be

Here is a civilised place for a coffee in Knokke. You sit at old worn tables surrounded by an odd assortment of cabinets, lamps and odd statues. Everything you see around you is for sale. Yet it feels like a comfortable living room.

113 BELGIUM PIER BRASSERIE
   Zeedijk 261
   Blankenberge
   Belgian Coast
   +32 (0)50 43 37 50
   www.belgiumpier.be

The round pavilion on Blankenberge Pier serves good coffee. But that is not the main reason to walk to the end of the pier. You come here for the stunning view of the North Sea through the huge curved windows. Or you come to sit out on the wooden deck if it is not blowing a gale.

114 'T GROOTE HUYS

**Karel
Janssenslaan 10
Ostend
Belgian Coast
+32 (0)59 70 10 67**
www.tgrootehuys.be

This is a striking 1891 house from the days when Ostend was one of the most elegant resorts in Europe. The interior is decorated in Flemish Renaissance style with high ceilings, wood panelling and big oak cupboards. You can come here in the afternoon to drink coffee in a shady secret garden.

115 DE MARÉ

**Kustlaan 119
Knokke
Belgian Coast
+32 (0)50 61 13 14**

Wieland Baert and An Baute run this traditional bakery and coffee shop in the heart of Knokke. You can sit out on the terrace on a bright metal chair for an early morning coffee and croissant, or settle inside on a rainy afternoon to eat a tasty little strawberry tart.

113 BELGIUM PIER BRASSERIE

111 DU PARC

The 5 best places to
DRINK A BELGIAN BEER
in Ostend

---

116 CAFÉ MANUSCRIPT
Langestraat 23
Ostend
Belgian Coast
www.manuscript
oostende.be

This is an appealing brown café with an old wood interior and an ancient piano standing on a small stage at the back. It opened in Ostend in 1991 and has evolved into a specialised beer café with some 70 bottled beers on offer. The list includes the distinctive Zinne Bir from Brasserie de la Senne and the complex abbey ale Sint-Bernardus Abt 12. The bar organises monthly concerts by new Belgian bands.

117 CAFÉ BOTTELTJE
Louisastraat 19
Ostend
Belgian Coast
+32 (0)59 70 09 28
www.hotelmarion.be

Here is a friendly Ostend bar attached to the Hotel Marion with an old wood floor, metal hanging lamps and a round bar where you can perch on a stool. With more than 300 bottled beers lined up at the back of the bar, this is one of the best places on the coast to discover Belgian specialities like Kwak, Brugse Zot or Ostend's own Keyte Tripel.

118 LAFAYETTE MUSICBAR

Langestraat 12
Ostend
Belgian Coast

This is a lively bar decorated with small red formica tables, wood panelling and photos of jazz musicians. It has a list of about 50 beers that include some rare lambics and even, if you are very lucky, Westvleteren. The music gets louder as the evening wears on until at some point someone will get up to dance between the tables.

119 POSEIDON

Hertstraat 11
Ostend
Belgian Coast
+32 (0)59 43 90 69
www.poseidon-oostende.be

You might easily walk straight past this café, but it is worth taking a look inside. The owner is a serious chef who creates simple Flemish cooking, including a delicious bouillabaisse using fresh fish from the North Sea. He also keeps more than 75 different beers behind the bar including craft beers from the Dolle Brouwers and occasionally a crate of bottles shipped from those difficult monks out at Westvleteren.

120 DE CRAYON

Kadzandstraat 10
Ostend
Belgian Coast

This relaxed music bar is one of Ostend's best-kept secrets. Once an artist's haunt, it has a bohemian atmosphere with bare brick walls and a faded mural of Ostend harbour. The owners organise free concerts by indie bands and occasional art exhibitions to keep the bohemian spirit alive. They also keep some good beers on tap including De Koninck and La Chouffe.

The 5 best
BEACH BARS

---

121 TWINS CLUB
Driftweg 39
Bredene
Belgian Coast
+32 (0)59 32 03 13
www.twinsclub.be

This beach bar in the dunes is different from other spots along the coast. It's a young, friendly place with three wooden decks where you can sit out in the sun watching the surfers. The bar attracts a mix of people from couples walking their dog to cyclists heading along the coast route. Parents can sit here while their children mess around in the sand.

122 SCHILDIA
Zeedijk 250
Knokke
Belgian Coast
+32 (0)50 51 50 58
www.schildia.be

This smart new beach bar opened in 2012. You can sit out in the summer months on a white deckchair with your feet in the sand. It feels almost tropical sitting under the palm trees with a cold Hoegaarden beer.

123 SIESTA BEACH
Zeedijk 700
Knokke
Belgian Coast
+32 (0)474 37 38 68
siestabeach.be

Siesta Beach has evolved over the years from a cluster of deckchairs and a beer stand into a cool lounge bar with smart white furniture and a pétanque court. It used to hold wild parties, but it's now a place to sit with a gin and tonic reading a summer novel.

124 CHALET WESTHINDER

Westdijk
Wenduine
Belgian Coast
+32 (0)50 41 58 55
westhinder.be

Hidden in the dunes near Wenduine, this simple wooden fisherman's cabin is one of the most romantic spots on the Belgian coast. You can reach it by following the coast footpath from De Haan to Wenduine. It is plain inside, with bare wooden tables and maritime relics. Or you can sit out on the terrace if the wind is not blowing sand in your face.

125 MONROE BEACH

OPPOSITE:
Zeedijk 711
Knokke
Belgian Coast
www.monroebeach.be

Here is one of the most chic beach bars on the coast. It is decorated in a lounge style with broad boardwalks, white umbrellas and gentle house music playing in the background. It could almost be Saint-Tropez.

121 TWINS CLUB

The 5 coolest spots for
COCKTAILS
at the coast

---

126 THE PHARMACY
Knokke
Belgian Coast
+32 (0)468 20 54 59

Jan van Ongevalle and his daughter Hannah run a mysterious cocktail bar in a secret location in Knokke. It's a classy place decorated like an eccentric private salon with dim lamps, old clocks and an animal skeleton in a glass case. It attracts a glamorous crowd including fashion models and actors. They come for the cool, friendly mood and the fantastic drinks. Phone ahead to book a table and get the address.

127 L'APEREAU
De Smet de Naeyer-laan 53
Blankenberge
Belgian Coast
+32 (0)475 23 90 39
www.lapereau.be

Blankenberge is slowly shaking off its tacky seaside image. Here is the proof. L'Apereau is a dazzling cocktail bar with a cool lounge interior and nostalgic views of old Blankenberge along one wall. The drinks are made by Jeroen Van Hecke who has created some very unusual cocktails and won several prizes.

128 NIGHTSHOP

Nellenstraat 134
Knokke
Belgian Coast

Every summer, art curators Delphine Bekaert and Jan Hoet Junior create a pop up gallery in an old abandoned villa next to Knokke Casino. They invite artists, musicians and designers to show off their creativity while serving cocktails and food until late. It's possibly the coolest spot on the coast for just a few weeks. Find out the dates on their Facebook page.

129 HEMMINGWAY

Langestraat 15
Ostend
Belgian Coast

Hemmingway is a new cocktail bar in the heart of Ostend's drinking district. It is decorated in a dark night club style with images of Hemmingway and Castro projected on screens at the back. You can sit at the bar with a Margarita or pick something more original from the list of 30 cocktails. But it's a noisy spot most nights, especially when there's a free party.

130 ROOD

Van Iseghemlaan
87-89
Ostend
Belgian Coast
www.rood-oostende.be

This corner café is a trendy spot to sit with a cocktail or a glass of white wine. Located in a striking 19th century building near the casino, it attracts a friendly mix of locals and tourists.

The 5 best
LOCAL BEERS
from independent breweries

---

131 WESTVLETEREN 12

Abdij Sint-Sixtus
Donkerstraat 12
Westvleteren
Flanders Fields
+32 (0)57 40 03 77
www.sintsixtus.be

The Trappist monks of Sint-Sixtus Abbey quietly brew some of the world's finest beers, including Westvleteren 12. But they only produce a few thousand bottles every year, making Westvleteren almost impossible to track down. It is sold at the abbey shop, although you have to phone in advance to reserve a crate. It's a complicated business, but worth it.

132 STRUISE PANNEPOT

De Struise Brouwers
www.struise.com

This is a sophisticated dark brown West Flanders ale launched by a small craft brewery in 2005. It takes its name from the fishing boats that used to sail from the port of De Panne. But it is a hard beer to find in Belgian cafés.

133 SINT-BERNARDUS ABT 12

This is a classic dark brown abbey beer served in a wide glass shaped like a chalice. Brewed less than 10 kilometres from the famous Westvleteren 12, it tastes very similar. Some beer drinkers even say that Sint-Bernardus is better. It is certainly much easier to get hold of a bottle.

134 POPERINGS HOMMELBIER

This is a subtle, complex beer with a mellow taste of Flemish hops. It is brewed in the Van Eecke family brewery in the village of Watou. This is the perfect beer to drink on a hot day after a cycle ride through the hop fields of West Flanders.

135 OERBIER

Roeselarestraat 12
Esen
Flanders Fields
+32 (0)51 50 27 81

A captivating craft beer produced in limited quantities by the passionate brewers who call themselves *De Dolle Brouwers* (The Mad Brewers). This is a serious strong amber ale made with Poperinge hops and then aged for some time in cold cellars.

131 WESTVLETEREN 12

L'AMUZETTE

25 PLACES TO SHOP

———

The 5 most **INSPIRING SHOPS** *at the coast* —— 74

The 5 best **FASHION SHOPS** *at the coast* —— 76

The 5 best **BIKE RENTAL SHOPS** —————— 78

The 5 best **DESIGN SHOPS** *at the coast* —— 80

The 5 best **INDEPENDENT BOOKSHOPS** —— 82

The 5 most
INSPIRING SHOPS
at the coast

---

136 **DE KARAVAAN**
Leopold II
Laan 213 W3
Oostduinkerke
Belgian Coast
+32 (0)58 62 07 25

Here is a cool shop filled with fun retro clothes and accessories. It sells flowery dresses by Edith & Ella like the ones your grandmother wore to the beach many decades ago. It also stocks an inspiring range of cute accessories, wooden toys and odd gadgets that no one honestly needs, like retro pinhole cameras.

137 **CALLEBERT**
Kustlaan 177
Knokke
Belgian Coast
+32 (0)50 62 75 55
www.callebert.be

This cool contemporary design shop opened in Knokke in 2005. It sells a small range of sleek functional objects by Danish and Italian companies, including Georg Jensen cutlery and Alessi cookware.

138 **FABIAAN VAN SEVEREN**
Vlaanderenstraat 68
Ostend
Belgian Coast
+32 (0)477 36 42 19
www.fabiaan vanseveren.be

Ostend designer Fabiaan Van Severen runs the most inspiring design store in Ostend. The son of a Belgian abstract artist, he started out painting before turning to furniture design. He now has a showroom where he sells his famous Crossed Legs Chair, as well as sofas, lamps and handbags.

139 L'AMUZETTE

Albertlaan 25
Knokke
Belgian Coast
+32 (0)50 69 12 44
www.lamuzette.be

This is a tiny concept store with walls that still have traces of old pink paint and torn wallpaper. The owner sells books, fashion accessories and bits and pieces for the kitchen. She also serves good coffee along with tasty cakes made by Julie's House in Ghent.

140 GALERIE BEAU SITE

Albert I-
promenade 39
Ostend
Belgian Coast
+32 (0)59 27 85 19
www.galeriebeausite.com

This is a striking new place on the Ostend promenade with a grand Art Deco interior on two floors and sweeping views of the sea. The owners have come up with an ambitious concept that combines art, design and food. The food is not quite right yet, but the art and design are interesting. You can sit on the terrace with a glass of chilled white wine while cool jazz plays in the background.

140 GALERIE BEAU SITE

139 L'AMUZETTE

The 5 best
FASHION SHOPS
at the coast

---

141 NR12

Lombardsijde-
straat 12
Nieuwpoort
Belgian Coast
+32 (0)58 24 14 04
www.nr12.be

Joëlle Swart and her brother opened this cool minimalist shop near Nieuwpoort beach in 2013. It has an inspiring selection of designer labels that are not easy to find anywhere else in Belgium, including dresses by the hot Spanish label Oky Coky and bright scarves for windy days at the beach by Plomo O Plata of Germany.

142 FERRER

Albert I laan 257
Nieuwpoort-Bad
Belgian Coast
+32 (0)58 23 23 09
www.ferrer.be

Carla Ferrer and her husband opened this boutique in Nieuwpoort in 2008. The exotic interior was designed by Studio Arne Quinze. Ferrer sells upmarket clothes by brands like Natan, See by Chloé and Marc by Marc Jacobs, along with perfumes by Juliette Has A Gun.

143 OBELISK

Albert I Laan 95
Oostduinkerke
Belgian Coast
+32 (0)58 52 06 59
www.obelisk-fashion.be

This is a relaxed store where you find cool fashions for men and women. You find smart dresses by creative Belgian designers like Tim Van Steenbergen, Sofie D'Hoore and A.F. Vandevorst, along with stylish scarves for a windy walk on the beach by Faliero Sarti.

144 PIED DE POULE

Rogierlaan 62
Ostend
Belgian Coast
+32 (0)59 43 54 51
www.pieddepoule
super.be

This is a stylish Ostend shop aimed at women looking for a relaxed look. It stocks the freshest fashions by cool French and Belgian labels like Isabel Marant Etoile, See by Chloé, Ba&sh and Filles à Papa.

145 BLUEPOINT

Antoine Breart-
straat 14
Knokke
+32 (0)50 70 51 58
www.bluepointstore.be

This small minimalist store located in a quiet side street attracts Knokke fashionistas with its stock of cool fashion labels, like Paul Smith, Sessun and American Vintage. It also has a collection of trendy T-shirts by Filles à Papa and Zoe Karssen for hot nights at the beach.

141 NR12

The 5 best
BIKE RENTAL SHOPS

146 CHEZ MARIE

Neermarkt 6
Ypres
Flanders Fields
+32 (0)57 20 02 06

Mieke Merlevede opened a shop with a warm interior of red brick and pale wood in 2014. Located opposite the cloth hall in Ypres, the shop rents out smart new bikes including electric bikes and tandems. Mieke also sells local beers like Hommelbier, Sint-Bernardus and Papegaei, as well as Hoorens coffee in stylish packs decorated by the Belgian artist Panamarenko.

147 ZONNEBEKE BIKES

Ieperstraat 19
Zonnebeke
Flanders Fields
+32 (0)472 23 54 58
www.zonnebekebikes.be

Koen rents out sturdy city bikes and tandems in a smart shop in the centre of Zonnebeke. You can pick up a bike for half a day to cycle out the old railway line to Tyne Cot Cemetery, or hold onto it for several days if you want to cycle along the Ypres Salient. Koen can tell you the best places to stop for lunch or even where to go bowling in Passendale.

148 **CATTRYSSE**

Leopoldlaan 16
De Haan
Belgian Coast
+32 (0)59 23 79 59
www.cattrysse.be

This bike shop has been run by the Cattrysse family for more than 70 years. The pavement outside is crammed with bright go-karts that can carry six people. But they also rent out serious bikes and tandems for cycle trips along the coast.

149 **CALIMERO**

Zeedijk 224
Koksijde
Belgian Coast
+32 (0)496 40 09 40
*www.verhuring
calimero.be*

You might wonder if you have come to the right place when you see the rows of bright go-karts parked outside this shop. But Calimero also rents out city bikes, tandems and electric bikes. You can rent a bike for a day to take a trip through the dunes into France.

150 **ROLLYWOOD**

Zeedijk 259
Knokke
Belgian Coast
+32 (0)50 51 11 48
www.rollywood.be

Here is a good address to pick up a sturdy Belgian city bike for a trip through the Zwin nature reserve. Located on the promenade in Heist, the shop stocks a wide range of models, including tandems and electric bikes.

The 5 best
DESIGN SHOPS
at the coast

---

151 DESIGN CLINIC
Albert I Laan 51
Oostduinkerke
Belgian Coast
+32 (0)58 51 61 33
www.designclinic.be

Here is an inspiring interior design store where young Belgian couples shop for cool furniture to fit out their new beach home. The shop carries several hip brands including Normann Copenhagen, Hay and Established & Sons.

152 WHITE INTERIORS
Langestraat 55
Ostend
Belgian Coast
+32 (0)477 17 57 30
www.whiteinteriors.be

This store sells some very cool vintage design in a vast white showroom close to the beach. The owner hunts out Scandinavian and American design classics of the 1950s and 1960s that could fit perfectly in a modern seaside apartment.

153 COULEUR LOCALE
Lippenslaan 275
Knokke
Belgian Coast
+32 (0)50 69 43 04
www.couleurlocale.eu

This relaxed design store sells an eclectic mix of objects including items that the owners have spotted in local markets during their travels across Africa. You find beautiful wooden pots, woven baskets and leather bracelets displaced in a casual bohemian setting.

154 LOFT LIVING

Lombardsijde-
straat 12
Nieuwpoort
Belgian Coast
+32 (0)58 24 09 02
www.loftliving.be

The trendy people of Nieuwpoort come to this smart design store near the seafront to pick up sofas and tables by brands like Tom Dixon, Vitra and Hay. The shop also stocks beautiful outdoor furniture by Tribù.

155 BEA ITEMS

Kustlaan 289
Knokke
Belgian Coast
+32 (0)50 60 36 06
www.items-knokke.com

Bea Mombaers runs a small store in Knokke where she displays exquisite vintage furniture, along with striped cushions, pots and modern paintings. People come here to get inspiring interior ideas for decorating their apartment at the coast.

153 COULEUR LOCALE

The 5 best
INDEPENDENT
BOOKSHOPS

156 CORMAN

Witte Nonnen-
straat 38
Ostend
Belgian Coast
+32 (0)59 70 27 24

Corman is a legendary Ostend bookstore
founded in 1925 by the flamboyant
globetrotting writer Mathieu Corman.
His bookshop in Adolf Buylstraat was
once, a long time ago, a favourite
meeting place for writers and artists
staying on the Belgian coast. It moved
to a new address in 1996, but still has
a warm literary atmosphere, with novels
and non-fiction on the shelves in French,
Dutch and English.

157 CORMAN BY FILIGRANES

Zeedijk 777
Knokke
Belgian Coast
+32 (0)50 60 18 28
*www.corman
byfiligranes.be*

This stylish modern bookstore on the
seafront in Het Zoute was recently taken
over by the Brussels bookshop Filigranes.
People come here to pick up a novel
for the beach, or something to read to
the children at bedtime. Most of the
books are in French, but you find some
contemporary English novels at the
back. It's worth climbing to the upper
floor where the art books are kept for
the sweeping view of the sea.

158 IN FLANDERS FIELDS MUSEUM SHOP

Grote Markt 34
Ypres
Flanders Fields
+32 (0)57 23 92 20
www.inflandersfields.be

The In Flanders Fields museum shop has an outstanding collection of books on the First World War, including military histories, novels, poetry collections and guidebooks. You can also pick up excellent maps for cycling or walking in the area.

159 THE BRITISH GRENADIER BOOKSHOP

Menenstraat 5
Ypres
Flanders Fields
+32 (0)57 21 46 57
www.salienttours.be

This is a neat bookshop on the road to the Menin Gate with a large collection of books and videos on the First World War. It also sells shiny brass shells, glass bottles salvaged from the battlefields, and wooden boxes filled with mysterious bits of rusting equipment. The shop is the starting point for bus tours run by Salient Tours.

160 OVER THE TOP TOURS BOOKSHOP

Menenstraat 41
Ypres
Flanders Fields
+32 (0)57 42 43 20
www.overthetoptours.be

This cluttered bookshop near the Menin Gate stocks an impressive collection of books on the war, along with a back room filled with rusting helmets and defused grenades. You can also buy old postcards of Ypres and book battlefield tours run by the owner.

LONE TREE CEMETERY

120 PLACES TO DISCOVER THE FIRST WORLD WAR

The 5 outstanding NEW VISITORS' CENTRES
in Flanders Fields ———————————— 88

The 5 most STRIKING NEW FEATURES
at In Flanders Fields Museum ———————— 91

The 5 most HISTORIC SITES in Ypres ————— 93

The 5 places to experience history
on the YPRES RAMPARTS ————————— 96

The 5 most CURIOUS DETAILS in Ypres ———— 98

The 5 most UNEXPECTED PLACES
in Poperinge ———————————————— 100

The 5 best TOURS ———————————————— 102

The 5 most HAUNTING CEMETERIES ———— 104

The 5 strangest GRAVESTONES ——————— 107

The 5 SMALLEST CEMETERIES ——————— 109

The 5 STRANGEST SIGHTS ——————— 111

The 5 most FORGOTTEN CEMETERIES ——— 113

The 5 most SECRET PLACES ——————— 115

The 5 most IMPRESSIVE TRENCHES ——— 117

The 5 most important DATES IN THE WAR — 119

The 5 largest CRATERS ———————— 121

The 5 most MEMORABLE CEREMONIES —— 124

The 5 most haunting VANISHED PLACES —— 127

The 5 most INSPIRING WALKS
in Flanders Fields ———————————— 129

The 5 ODDEST PLACE NAMES —————— 131

The 5 BEST FILMS *on Flanders Fields* ——— 133

The 5 most STRIKING ART WORKS ——— 135

The 5 most unusual WAR MEMORIALS ——— 137

The 5 best BOOKS TO READ
about Flanders Fields———————————— 140

The 5 outstanding
NEW VISITORS'
CENTRES *in Flanders Fields*

---

161 IN FLANDERS FIELDS MUSEUM

Grote Markt 34
Ypres
Flanders Fields
+32 (0)57 23 92 20
www.inflandersfields.be

This inspiring war museum is located in the vast mediaeval cloth hall in Ypres. It contains many relics of the First World War, including weapons, uniforms and personal objects. But its main aim is to tell the personal stories of people caught up in the conflict and to show the lingering traces of the First World War in the landscape around Ypres.

162 LIJSSENTHOEK CEMETERY

Boescheepseweg 35A
Poperinge
Flanders Fields
+32 (0)57 22 36 36
www.lijssenthoek.be

This huge military cemetery contains almost 11,000 graves from 30 different countries. It stands in the fields near Poperinge where several hospitals were located during the war. The visitor pavilion was added in 2012 by the architect Luc Vandewynckel in the style of the wooden huts where soldiers were treated. It contains a fascinating exhibition on the doctors and nurses who worked here.

161 IN FLANDERS FIELDS MUSEUM

164 TYNE COT

163 PASSCHENDAELE MEMORIAL MUSEUM

Berten Pilstraat 5A
Zonnebeke
Flanders Fields
+32 (0)51 77 04 41
www.passchendaele.be

An outstanding new war museum opened in 2013 in a reconstructed manor house in the village of Zonnebeke. It tells the story of the war in a series of dark rooms on the first floor filled with uniforms, old diaries and photographs. But the most impressive section of the museum lies deep underground where you can wander through a vast reconstructed dugout while shells seem to be exploding above your head.

164 TYNE COT

Tynecotstraat 22
Passendale
Flanders Fields

Tyne Cot Cemetery is the largest British military cemetery in the world, with 12,000 graves and a further 35,000 names of missing soldiers carved on a long wall at the back. As you approach, you hear a haunting woman's voice slowly recite the names of the dead. You then enter a simple modern pavilion designed by the architects Govaert & Vanhoutte in 2006 with a glass wall that looks out across the battlefield.

165 LANGEMARK

Klerkenstraat
Langemark
Flanders Fields

The huge German cemetery at Langemark is entered by a sober black pavilion designed by architects Govaert & Vanhoutte. Here you can watch historical films on three screens before entering the cemetery along a path lined with willows. This is a dark and somber place with flat grave stones and rugged stone crosses. Many of the dead were young students who joined the German army in the early years of the war.

The 5 most **STRIKING NEW FEATURES**
at *In Flanders Fields Museum*

IN FLANDERS FIELDS MUSEUM
Grote Markt 34
Ypres
Flanders Fields
+32 (0)57 23 92 20
www.inflandersfields.be

166 TINDERSTICKS SOUNDTRACK

The In Flanders Fields Museum was totally redesigned in 2013 to shift the emphasis from the experience of war to the impact on the landscape. The new presentation incorporates a strange instrumental soundtrack composed by the British indie band Tindersticks after a visit to Vladslo German Cemetery.

167 POPPY BRACELET

Everyone gets a bright plastic bracelet to wear while they visit the museum. It uses digital technology to match you up with four individuals who were caught up in the war as soldiers or civilians. You gradually learn their stories as you move through the museum.

168 FLANDERS EARTH

This striking video presentation projects old army maps onto a screen alongside recent Google Earth images showing the same spots. Its aim is to show how the landscape around Ypres has slowly changed over the years as trenches and mud are replaced by fields and cemeteries.

169 ELVERDINGE TREE TRUNK

One of the biggest surprises in the new museum is a section of tree trunk cut from an oak tree felled in 1994. The ancient tree used to grow in the grounds of Elverdinge Castle in an area that was heavily shelled during the war. When it was cut down, traces of burning could be seen in the rings dating from 1914 to 1918.

170 PASSCHENDAELE FILM

The Battle of Passchendaele is presented in a new film screened in an auditorium. It provides short film portraits of some of the people who worked in the hospitals behind the lines where they treated thousands of wounded soldiers.

The 5 most
HISTORIC SITES
in Ypres

---

171 MENIN GATE

Meninstraat
Ypres
Flanders Fields

Nothing prepares you for the Menin Gate. This huge limestone arch on the edge of the old town is carved with the names of 54,896 soldiers. These are the names of the soldiers whose bodies vanished in the Ypres battlefields. It is not even all of them. There are a further 35,000 names on a wall at Tyne Cot cemetery and more names on other monuments, making a total of 102,000 bodies that were never recovered.

172 ST GEORGE'S MEMORIAL CHURCH

Elverdingsestraat 1
Ypres
Flanders Fields

St George's Memorial Church was built in 1928 for the war pilgrims visiting Ypres, as well as the 600 or so British people who settled in the town after the war. Designed by Reginald Blomfield, it is modelled on a traditional English parish church. The interior is crammed with touching memorials including little brass plaques on the backs of chairs.

171_ MENIN GATE

173 ETON MEMORIAL SCHOOL

Elverdingsestraat 1
Ypres
Flanders Fields

No plaque. Nothing. The tiny Eton Memorial School lies hidden behind a brick wall next to the St George's Memorial Church. It was built by Eton School in 1929 in memory of 342 former students who died during the war. The school served the small British community that had settled in Ypres after the war, including the children of gardeners who looked after the war cemeteries. But it was evacuated in 1940 and the children never came back.

174 LAPIDARIUM

Vandenpeereboom-plein
Ypres
Flanders Fields

Not many people walk around the back of the Cathedral to look at the ruined cloister. The abandoned garden is dotted with fragments of architecture and sculpture from buildings destroyed in the war. Nothing is labeled. These are fragments of a lost city.

175 ST MARTIN'S CATHEDRAL

Sint-Maartensplein
Ypres
Flanders Fields

The Cathedral was destroyed in the First World War, but rebuilt in the 1920s in the original Gothic style. Now you would hardly know that it was once a pile of rubble. It contains some war memorials and an impressive painting of the Siege of Ypres of 1383.

The 5 places
to experience history on the
YPRES RAMPARTS

—————

176 POEDERTOREN
Esplanade
Ypres
Flanders Fields

You can go on a fascinating walk around the Ypres ramparts from the station to the Menin Gate. On the way, you pass several buildings from different periods, such as the massive stone *Poedertoren* near the railway station that was once used to store gunpowder.

177 PILL BOXES
Esplanade
Ypres
Flanders Fields

Two concrete pill boxes from World War One can still be seen on the ramparts. They were built by British troops to protect the city from a possible attack.

178 RAMPARTS CEMETERY
Rijsselstraat
Ypres
Flanders Fields

A beautiful cemetery was built on sloping land on the edge of the moat. It has just 193 graves, including six from the New Zealand Maori Battalion at the far end and six Australian soldiers killed by a single shell. The writer Rose Coombs, who wrote a guide to the Ypres battlefields in 1976, was particularly fond of this cemetery. Her ashes were scattered here after she died in 1991.

179 **PREDIKHERENTOREN**
Arsenaalstraat
Ypres
Flanders Fields

This is the base of a massive round tower built in the 14th century during the Burgundian period. You can still enter the underground foundations through a long brick tunnel.

180 **POTERNE STAIRCASE**
ENTRANCE OPPOSITE:
Sint-Jacobsstraat 66
Ypres
Flanders Fields

You could easily miss the flight of stone steps that lead down from the ramparts to the moat. Built in the 17th century, they were part of a secret network of tunnels and stairs used to defend the city.

177 PILL BOXES

The 5 most
CURIOUS DETAILS
in Ypres

---

181 ALBERT AND ELISABETH STATUES

Grote Markt 34
Ypres
Flanders Fields

The ruined cloth hall was rebuilt between 1928 and 1967 in the original Gothic style. But there are some small details that are new, including the modern figures of King Albert and Queen Elisabeth placed in a niche at the foot of the belfry, next to the mediaeval figures of Boudewijn IX and Margaret of Champagne.

182 HAIG HOUSE ADVERTISING MURAL

Poperingseweg 55-56
Ypres
Flanders Fields

An intriguing blue and white painted advertising sign was uncovered on the side wall of a brick house in 2013. 'Visit Haig House Ypres,' it reads, 'For information and Haig poppy wreaths.' The sign was put up in the 1930s on the main road into Ypres from Poperinge to catch the attention of British tourists visiting the war cemeteries.

183 IEPER STRAND

Lange Torhoutstraat
Ypres
Flanders Fields

One of the strangest spots in Ypres is hidden behind a high brick wall near the Menin Gate. Once a modern open-air swimming pool, it is now abandoned. The changing cabins are derelict and you can even see fish swimming in the pool. The café is called, rather optimistically, Ypres Beach. It is a strange, forgotten spot where parents sit on the café terrace while their kids play in the sand.

184 PATRICIA COUTURE

Stationsstraat 55
Ypres
Flanders Fields

Two identical shops were built in 1926 on the street leading to the station. They have Art Deco façades typical of the 1920s and elegant interiors that have hardly changed. The shop on the right still has a wrought iron sign with the name Patricia Couture and old fashion prints in the window. But there is no hint of anyone inside.

185 STONE FOUNDATIONS

The houses of Ypres were carefully rebuilt after the war in their original style. It was as if people wanted to believe that the war never happened. But if you look carefully, you can sometimes see ancient stone foundations that survived the shelling.

The 5 most
UNEXPECTED PLACES
in Poperinge

---

186 TALBOT HOUSE
Gasthuisstraat 43
Poperinge
Flanders Fields
+32 (0)57 33 32 28
www.talbothouse.be

A strange old iron sign hangs outside a town house on the main street in Poperinge. It dates from the time when Poperinge was teeming with soldiers on leave. The house still has the beds where soldiers spent the night, an old piano and a strange temporary chapel in the attic.

187 DEATH CELLS
Guido Gezellestraat 1
Poperinge
Flanders Fields
www.toerisme
poperinge.be

It is easy to miss the red door at the side of Poperinge town hall. Push it open and go into the courtyard. Here you can see the spot where 15 British and two Canadian soldiers were executed at dawn.

188 REKHOF CEMETERY
Rekhof
Poperinge
Flanders Fields

The old town cemetery in Poperinge is a romantic, overgrown place created in 1794 on the site of a hop field. It contains magnificent 19th century graves, along with some sad memorials to children who died young. Dotted around the old graves are clean white gravestones belonging to British soldiers who died in Poperinge in the early months of the war.

189 HOTEL SKINDLES

Gasthuisstraat 57
Poperinge
Flanders Fields

The grand 18th century town house
called Hotel Skindles was once owned by
a rich Poperinge family. During the war,
it became an officers' club named after
the famous Skindles Hotel on the River
Thames in Maidenhead. Soon after the
war ended, it was turned into a hotel for
war pilgrims visiting the cemeteries.
The building now lies empty.

190 WEEUWHOF

Sint-Annastraat 7
Poperinge
Flanders Fields

A series of neat 18th century Flemish
almshouses stand on a narrow lane
in Poperinge. They were built on the
site of a hop garden to provide homes
for 12 poor widows over the age of 70.
A small door leads into a secluded
garden surrounded by whitewashed
almshouses now owned by the local
social welfare department.

186 TALBOT HOUSE

The 5 best
TOURS

---

191 RENT A GUIDE
+32 (0)488 40 74 40
rentaguide.be

Miguel Bouttry runs a small company that offers personal guided tours of Flanders Fields. He picks up small groups in his minivan and drives them out to sites around the battlefields. He knows the region intimately and can track down a particular relative's grave and research the story of how he was killed.

192 FLANDERS BATTLEFIELD TOURS
Slachthuisstraat 58
Ypres
Flanders Fields
+32 (0)57 36 04 60
www.ypres-fbt.com

Jacques Ryckebosch used to welcome visitors to Talbot House in Poperinge. Now he takes small groups on guided tours of the Ypres battlefields. If you provide him with a name, he can research the individual's story and put together a personal tour.

193 SALIENT TOURS
Menenstraat 5
Ypres
Flanders Fields
+32 (0)57 21 46 57
www.salienttours.be

Salient Tours organise tours of the battlefields starting from The British Grenadier Bookshop. They have been running minibus tours for small groups since 1998 and know every war cemetery in the region.

194 **FRONTLINE TOURS**

Grote Markt 1
Ypres
Flanders Fields
+32 (0)57 85 99 35
+32 (0)474 36 76 08
www.frontline-tours.com

Lionel is a passionate local guide who takes small groups around the battlefields and cemeteries in a Mercedes minibus. He is a flexible and friendly storyteller with an intimate knowledge of every back road and small cemetery. His stock of old photographs and military maps adds to the experience. Children in particular like his informal approach.

195 **DE LIJN BUS 14**

www.delijn.be

A new regular bus service was launched by the transport company De Lijn in 2014 to link several important World War One towns, including Nieuwpoort, Diksmuide and Ypres. A Poppy Day Pass allows you to use the entire West Flanders network for a day, including bus 14.

WW I CEMETERIES

The 5 most
HAUNTING
CEMETERIES

196 HEDGE ROW TRENCH CEMETERY

Verbrandemolen-
straat
Zillebeke
Flanders Fields

This is possibly the most beautiful of all the cemeteries in Flanders Fields. Hidden in the Palingbeek woods, it is a silent, mysterious place that can only be reached along a forest track. The original cemetery was destroyed by shellfire and the graves were laid out after the war in a circle. Three army packs are lined up mysteriously outside the wall. They contain objects that soldiers once carried, like gas masks, handkerchiefs and even make-up.

197 RIFLE HOUSE CEMETERY

Rue Saint-Yvon
Ploegsteert
Flanders Fields

Located in the depths of Ploegsteert wood, this is one of the most remote of the war cemeteries. It can only be reached on foot along a dark forest trail that ends at this silent spot. One of the graves belongs to a young Jewish boy called R. Barnett who was just 15 when he died on 19 December 1914.

198 LONE TREE CEMETERY

199 SPANBROEKMOLEN CEMETERY

197 RIFLE HOUSE CEMETERY

198 LONE TREE CEMETERY

Kruisstraat
Wijtschate
Flanders Fields

A narrow concrete path runs across a field next to a farm on the Messines Ridge. It leads to a little walled cemetery just beyond a clump of trees. Most of the soldiers buried here came from Ulster. They left the trenches a few seconds too early on the morning of 7 June 1917 and were killed instantly when the Spanbroekmolen mine went off at 3.10 am.

199 SPANBROEKMOLEN CEMETERY

Kruisstraat
Wijtschate
Flanders Fields

This remote little cemetery is reached by a path across a field. It is a quiet spot where almost no one comes. The Irish soldiers buried here died on the same day as their comrades at Lone Tree Cemetery. They were wiped out by machine gun fire after they left the trenches too early.

200 VLADSLO CEMETERY

Houtlandstraat
Diksmuide
Flanders Fields

This huge German cemetery lies on a quiet road in the middle of the Praetbos woods. Planted with oak trees, it is a quiet and melancholy place. More than 25,000 soldiers are buried here, yet you might be the only visitor. The names are carved in small letters on stones that lie flat on the ground. There are no personal details, nothing to say who they were, or where they died.

The 5 strangest
GRAVESTONES

---

201 WILLIE REDMOND
Godtschalckstraat 3
Loker
Flanders Fields

Major William Redmond lies buried in an isolated grave outside the walls of Locre Hospice Cemetery. A popular Irish nationalist politician, he was wounded in the dawn attack on Messines Ridge on 7 June 1917 and treated at a Catholic hospice. He died later that day and was buried in the convent garden in a grave that was later covered with flowers. The convent was destroyed by shellfire in 1918 but this grave miraculously survived.

202 VALENTINE JOE STRUDWICK
Essex Farm Cemetery
Diksmuidseweg
Boezinge
Flanders Fields
Plot I, row U, grave 8

Not much is known about Valentine Joe Strudwick except that he was just 15 years old when he died. He was killed near Boezinge on the banks of the Yser canal on 14 January 1916. His grave in Essex Farm Cemetery is often buried under wreaths and small wooden crosses placed by children on school trips.

203 THE UNKNOWN SOLDIER

Deken De Bolaan 37
Poperinge
Flanders Fields

A small war cemetery lies hidden among modern houses on the road out of Poperinge. It was created on the site of a private garden, but soon became too small. The gravestones are all lined up at the back, apart from one solitary gravestone to an unknown soldier. It stands on its own with a single poppy growing in front. No one knows why it is there.

204 CHINESE GRAVES

Boescheepseweg 35A
Poperinge
Flanders Fields
www.lijssenthoek.be

The war cemetery at Lijssenthoek contains the graves of 35 men from the Chinese Labour Corps who died here, mainly during the 1919 Spanish flu epidemic. But 13 Chinese workers were killed on the night of 15 November 1917 at Busseboom camp when a German pilot spotted a cigarette glowing in the dark. Chinese people living in Belgium sometimes come here on Qing Ming, the day of the dead, to place small symbolic objects like cigarettes on the graves.

205 HERBERT MORRIS

Poperinge New
Military Cemetery
Deken de Bolaan 127
Poperinge
Flanders Fields
Plot II, row J, grave 34

Herbert Morris was a young Jamaican who lied about his age to join the army. He fled from the trenches during an attack because he could not stand the sound of gunfire. Morris was only 17 when he was sentenced to death for cowardice. He was the youngest of the 17 soldiers shot in the courtyard of Poperinge town hall.

The 5
SMALLEST
CEMETERIES

---

206 BETHLEHEM FARM EAST CEMETERY

Rijselstraat
Mesen
Flanders Fields

This cemetery on the Messines Ridge is the smallest in the area with just 44 graves. It takes its name from a German bunker where Adolf Hitler spent some time in 1917. The bunker was captured by Australians on 7 June 1917 and turned into a field hospital. Most of the soldiers buried here were killed in the June offensive.

207 BRIDGE HOUSE CEMETERY

OPPOSITE:
Roeselarestraat 11
Langemark
Flanders Fields

This small cemetery next to a little stream contains just 45 graves of British soldiers. All but one of them died between 26 and 28 September 1917 in the Battle of Polygon Wood. The cemetery takes its name from a farm fortified by the German army close to a bridge over the Steenbeek.

208 SUFFOLK CEMETERY

BEHIND:
Kriekstraat 16
Kemmel
Flanders Fields

This small, orderly cemetery lies in peaceful Flemish countryside to the south of Ypres. The cemetery contains 47 graves of soldiers mostly killed during the German Spring Offensive in 1918.

209 RED FARM CEMETERY

NEAR:
Poperingseweg 502
Vlamertinge
Flanders Fields

This little cemetery lies in the fields off the main road from Ypres to Poperinge. It was created in 1918 next to a field hospital named Red Farm that lay out of range of shellfire. Wounded soldiers were brought here for treatment during the Battle of the Lys in April 1918. The cemetery contains just 46 soldiers, along with three unidentified Belgian civilians buried in Row A.

210 COLNE VALLEY CEMETERY

Kleine Poezelstraat
Boezinge
Flanders Fields

This small cemetery to the north of Ypres is now surrounded by modern industrial buildings. It gets its romantic name from a trench that once ran parallel to the Ypres canal. The cemetery contains 47 graves of British soldiers who mainly died in the summer of 1915.

207 BRIDGE HOUSE CEMETERY

The 5
STRANGEST SIGHTS

211 AMERICAN HOUSE

Berten Pilstraat 5A
Zonnebeke
Flanders Fields
+32 (0)51 77 04 41

A curious wooden house was reconstructed in the grounds of the Zonnebeke museum in 2014. It was originally built in 1922 with American aid as a temporary home for Belgian refugees. The house was damaged in the Second World War, but remained occupied until 1978. The interior is filled with old furniture and eccentric possessions.

212 ZANDVOORDE BUNKER

Oude Zonnebekestraat
Zandvoorde
Flanders Fields

A path leads across a field to a crumbling German bunker with a carved stone on the outside giving the construction date of 1916. You can go inside the bunker and peer out through narrow windows at the Passchendaele battlefield.

213 1,392 POSTS

Boescheepseweg 35A
Poperinge
Flanders Fields
www.lijssenthoek.be

The hospital cemetery at Lijssenthoek is entered along a new footpath lined with 1,392 posts. The posts count out the days of the war and the number of soldiers who died in the hospital each day. You can see the major battles reflected in the rising number of deaths. But someone died here every day of the war.

214 VAN RAEMDONCK BROTHERS CHAPEL

Van Raemdonck-
straat
Zuidschote
Flanders Fields

One of the strangest monuments in Flanders Fields stands in a field near the road from Diksmuide to Ypres. It commemorates two Belgian brothers killed on 26 March 1917 in an attack on a German bunker. The story of the two brothers who died together became one of the most famous Belgian legends of the war. They were buried in the crypt of the IJzertoren memorial and commemorated by this massive monument built of concrete blocks salvaged from the bunker.

215 UNEXPLODED SHELLS

It hardly seems possible, but rusting shells are still being dug out of the Flanders soil, almost one hundred years after they were fired. Occasionally someone is killed when a shell explodes unexpectedly. It seems that the war is still not over in this corner of the world.

211 AMERICAN HOUSE

VIEW FROM THE IJZERTOREN

The 5 most
FORGOTTEN
CEMETERIES

---

216 PLOEGSTEERT WOOD
Rue Saint-Yvon
Ploegsteert
Flanders Fields

This is one of three cemeteries hidden deep in Ploegsteert Wood. It can only be reached on foot along a muddy forest track. It is a strange, silent place. Leslie Beauchamp, brother of the writer Katherine Mansfield, was buried here in October 1915 after a grenade blew up in his hand. 'Blown to bits!' according to his devastated sister.

217 POPERINGE OLD MILITARY CEMETERY
Deken De Bolaan
Poperinge
Flanders Fields

You can easily walk straight past this cemetery, which is hidden behind a house on the road out of Poperinge. The narrow path leads to a large empty lawn that looks almost like an English back garden. Some 427 soldiers are buried in long rows here, among the family houses.

218 BANDAGHEM CEMETERY
Nachtegaalstraat
Haringhe
Flanders Fields

Bandaghem Cemetery takes its name from a huge hospital built in the countryside to treat soldiers wounded in the Battle of Passchendaele. Not many people visit it because it lies a long way from the battlefields. The soldiers called the hospital Bandaghem as a joke, borrowing the ending 'hem' from the names of Flemish villages they had passed through. The nearby cemeteries of Dozinghem and Mendinghem were also given mock Flemish names.

219 HOOGLEDE CEMETERY

Beverenstraat 78
Hooglede
Flanders Fields

The German cemetery at Hooglede is the smallest of the four German cemeteries in Flanders Fields. It was abandoned and overgrown for many years, but volunteer gardeners from Germany have tidied it up in time for the 100th anniversary. A strange stone pavilion known as the Ehrenhall or Hall of Honour was built here using stones from the German pavilion at the 1928 Paris World Exhibition.

220 MENEN GERMAN CEMETERY

Groenestraat
Menen
Flanders Fields

The largest German war cemetery from the First World War lies hidden in trees near the town of Menen. It is a vast, somber cemetery that lies a long way from the main sites in Flanders Fields. More than 48,000 soldiers are buried here, many of them brought to hospitals outside Menen during the Battle of Passchendaele. This is the German equivalent of Tyne Cot, yet it is usually deserted.

The 5 most
SECRET PLACES

---

221 LA BASSECOUR
Armentiers-
steenweg 26
Mesen
Flanders Fields

Two of the 19 mines buried under the Messines Ridge failed to detonate on 7 June 1917. One exploded in the summer of 1955, but the other still lies buried deep underground. No one knows precisely where it lies, but it might well lie below a farm called La Bassecour on the main road from Mesen to Armentières. The farmer says he has no intention of moving.

222 MESEN CHURCH CRYPT
Sint-Niklaaskerk
Mesen
Flanders Fields

The church in Mesen was destroyed during the First World War, exposing a hidden Romanesque crypt. It was used by the German army as a field hospital during the war. Adolf Hitler was brought here after he was wounded and sat down to paint the ruined church during a break in the fighting.

223 THE IRISH WALL

Godtschalckstraat 3
Loker
Flanders Fields

Not many people notice the fragment of wall in a garden near Locre Hospice Cemetery. It was built by Irish workers in 1998 using stones left over from the Irish Peace Tower in Mesen. They added a dedication in English and Irish to Major William Redmond who died near here in 1917. It quotes his words: 'Don't go, but come with me.'

224 THE KEMMEL OAK TREE

Noordstraat
Kemmel
Flanders Fields

An ancient oak tree stands at a bend in the road to the west of Kemmel. It is one of the only trees that survived the war in this region.

225 THE LOKER OAK TREE

Lampernissestraat
Loker
Flanders Fields

A single solitary oak tree stands in a field behind Locre Hospice Cemetery. It was planted in the spring of 1984 by the widow of Jacques Covemaecker, a local farmer who was killed by an exploding shell on 23 May 1983. The tree stands on the spot where he was killed in the early evening while ploughing his land.

The 5 most
IMPRESSIVE
TRENCHES

---

226 BAYERNWALD

Voormezelestraat
Wijtschate
Flanders Fields

TICKETS SOLD AT:
Kemmel tourist
office
Sint-Laurentiusplein 1
Kemmel
Flanders Fields
+32 (0)57 45 04 55
www.heuvelland.be

Not many people visit Bayernwald Trenches, yet this is one of the most fascinating relics from the First World War. The trenches were constructed in 1916 by German troops along the high ground to the south of Ypres. The trenches were buried after the war, but in 1971 a local school teacher discovered two deep mines along with four concrete bunkers. The site was restored in 2004, although it is not the easiest place to visit as you first have to buy a ticket at Kemmel tourist office.

227 YORKSHIRE TRENCH

Bargiestraat
Ypres
Flanders Fields

This is a strange place hidden from view in the middle of a modern industrial estate. But it is worth heading out of Ypres along the right bank of the canal to track it down. The trenches here were excavated and reconstructed in the 1990s by a group called the Diggers. They discovered 155 bodies of British, German and French soldiers, along with dozens of relics now displayed at the In Flanders Fields Museum.

228 SANCTUARY WOOD
Canadalaan
Ypres
Flanders Fields

You can walk through an extensive network of trenches hidden in the woods behind the cluttered Hill 60 Museum. The trenches have been repaired over the years, but they still give some impression of the mud and damp of trench warfare, especially after heavy rainfall.

229 PASSCHENDAELE MEMORIAL MUSEUM
Berten Pilstraat 5A
Zonnebeke
Flanders Fields
+32 (0)51 77 04 41

A replica trench has been built in the grounds of Zonnebeke Castle. You can wander for a considerable distance and peer inside reconstructed dugouts.

230 DODENGANG
IJzerdijk 65
Diksmuide
Flanders Fields

A line of reconstructed trenches runs along the west bank of the River Yser near Diksmuide. Known as the Dodengang or Trench of Death, this was a dangerous spot in the Belgian line.

229 PASSCHENDAELE MEMORIAL MUSEUM

226 BAYERENWALD

The 5 most important
DATES IN THE WAR

---

231 19 OCTOBER 1914

On this day, General Erich von Falkenhayn launched the first in a series of savage attacks in an attempt to break through the British defences around Ypres. Thousands of young German students marched into battle through Langemark village singing patriotic songs. But many of them were killed almost immediately, like 17-year-old Pieter Kollwitz from Berlin. The Germans refer to this futile battle as the Massacre of the Innocents.

232 24 DECEMBER 1914

Chemin du Mont de la Hutte
Ploegsteert
Flanders Fields

On Christmas Eve 1914, an extraordinary event took place in the frozen trenches near Ploegsteert Wood. Soldiers on both sides stopped fighting and began to sing Christmas carols. Some climbed out of the trenches to bury the dead, shook hands with the enemy and exchanged little gifts. They also played a game of football in a cabbage field, which was won by the German side.

233 22 APRIL 1915

In the afternoon of 22 April, German troops opened the valves on gas cylinders dug into the trenches between Steenstraat and Langemark. They released a yellow cloud of poisonous chlorine gas that drifted towards trenches held by French and Algerian troops. The gas had been developed by a brilliant Jewish German scientist called Fritz Haber, whose wife Clara Immerwahr committed suicide in Berlin after learning of her husband's role.

234 7 JUNE 1917

On this day, a series of 19 secret underground mines were detonated along the Messines Ridge to the south of Ypres at 3.10 in the morning. The mines created the largest man-made explosion in history, so powerful that it rattled the chandeliers in Buckingham Palace. Soldiers from four countries then advanced through the shell holes and captured several German trenches.

235 31 JULY 1917

After ten days of bombardment by 3,000 guns, the Allied army launched an attack on the Passchendaele ridge on 31 July 1917. It quickly became a disaster due to heavy rain that turned the ground to deep mud. The fighting went on for thirteen weeks before the ridge was captured by Canadian troops. Many see this as one of the most futile battles in history, with 35 soldiers dying for every metre of land gained.

The 5 largest
CRATERS

---

236 SINT-ELOI CRATER

Rijselseweg
Voormezele
Flanders Fields

You can track down the remains of 16 craters along the Messines Ridge that were created by huge underground mines detonated at 3.10 am on 7 June 1917. The Sint-Eloi Crater was produced by the largest of the underground mines. It is now a quiet spot with an abandoned British bunker. Almost no one comes here, but you can enter the site by asking at the Ypres tourist office for an access code.

237 CATERPILLAR CRATER

Zwarteleenstraat
Zillebeke
Flanders Fields

A large remote crater is hidden in the Palingbeek woods near Hill 60. The crater, now filled with water, is close to the railway line between Ypres and Comines. It is a quiet spot where you hear only birdsong. You can reach the site on a forest trail by following the numbered signs 28 and 27.

237 CATERPILLAR CRATER

238 LONE TREE CRATER

238 LONE TREE CRATER

Kruisstraat
Wijtschate
Flanders Fields

The Lone Tree Crater was created by one of 19 underground mines that went off on 7 June 1917. It is now filled with water and hidden by trees. It became known as the Pool of Peace and was bought from the landowner as a peace memorial. Some fragments of a German bunker can still be seen in the undergrowth.

239 KRUISSTRAAT CRATER

Wulvergemstraat
Wulvergem
Flanders Fields

Two waterlogged craters stand in a field near the Pool of Peace. They were created by underground mines dug below the German trenches. Now they are used by local fishermen.

240 SAINT-YVON CRATERS

Riche Rue
Saint-Yvon
Flanders Fields

Two craters stand near a quiet country road not far from Ploegsteert Wood. They were detonated along with 17 others along the ridge that ran from Sanctuary Wood to Ploegsteert. The craters are now peaceful ponds surrounded by trees.

The 5 most
MEMORABLE CEREMONIES

---

241 MENIN GATE
Menin Gate
Ypres
Flanders Fields

There is nothing like this anywhere in the world. Every evening at just before 8 pm, the traffic is halted on Menenstraat in Ypres. Two local firemen then raise their shiny bugles to play the Last Post. This sad tune was first performed in Ypres at the unveiling of the Menin Gate on 24 July 1927. The local police chief was so moved that he set up a committee to ensure it was played every day. Huge, noisy crowds now gather under the gate every evening.

242 SPORTSMAN BAR
Hagebos
Flanders Fields

The Sportsman is a simple local café on the busy road from Ypres to Langemark. You could easily drive past without noticing it. But a unique ceremony is held here on the first Monday of every month to commemorate the Welsh poet Hedd Wyn who died across the road during the Battle of Pilckem Ridge. The event is organised by the café owner, who has also created a corner in the café in memory of Hedd Wyn.

241 MENIN GATE

243 IRISH TOWER

Armentierssteenweg
Mesen
Flanders Fields

The Island of Ireland Peace Tower is designed so that sunlight enters the interior at exactly 11 am on 11 November. The tower was unveiled on 11 November 1998 after a service held at 11 am. Every year, people gather at the tower at 11 am to mark the end of the war at the eleventh hour of the eleventh day of the eleventh month.

244 CREST FARM

Canadalaan 37
Zonnebeke
Flanders Fields

It is already dark at 6 pm on 10 November when Canadians and Belgians gather by torchlight at Crest Farm Memorial for a deeply moving ceremony. It is held to commemorate the Canadian troops who died in the attack on Passchendaele village.

245 FLANDERS FIELD AMERICAN CEMETERY

Waregem
Flanders Fields

A moving ceremony is held every year on Memorial Day (the last Monday in May) at the American war cemetery in Waregem. Begun in 1922, the ceremony involves children from the local school who sing the Star Spangled Banner and then place American and Belgian flags in front of the 368 graves.

The 5 most haunting
VANISHED PLACES

246 FRIEDHOF ROGGEVELD

Steenstraat
Diksmuide
Flanders Fields

No sign. Nothing. It just looks like an uneven meadow with some young trees. But this field near the café Roggeveld was once a German cemetery where 1,558 soldiers were buried under simple wooden crosses. One of them was Pieter Kollwitz who died near here on 23 October 1914. In 1954, the bodies were moved to Vladslo Cemetery, leaving nothing behind.

247 1955 MINE CRATER

Mesen
Flanders Fields

A huge explosion occurred on 17 June 1955 when an underground mine went off during a thunderstorm, killing a cow. It was one of two mines buried under the Messines Ridge that failed to detonate on 7 June 1917. The crater has now been filled with earth, leaving no trace of the explosion.

248 GAS ATTACK MONUMENT

Steenstraat
Boezinge
Flanders Fields

A huge aluminium cross stands next to the main road from Diksmuide to Ypres. It was put up in 1961 on the site of a 1929 monument in memory of French soldiers killed in the 1915 German gas attack. The monument was blown up by German troops in 1941 because it referred to German barbarity.

249 GARDEN

Elverdingestraat 1
Ypres
Flanders Fields

A narrow path next to the St George's Memorial Church leads to a hidden garden with a few wooden benches. This was once the school yard of the Eton Memorial School. But the school has gone. So have all the children. It is now a strangely silent spot in the heart of Ypres.

250 HAIG HOUSE

Korte Torhoutstraat
Ypres
Flanders Fields

Tourists visiting the war cemeteries used to be able to buy poppies at Haig House. It closed down in 1940 when the Germans invaded Belgium. All traces have vanished, except for an advertising sign on the side of a house on Poperingseweg.

The 5 most

INSPIRING WALKS

in Flanders Fields

---

251 YPRES TOWN WALLS
Menin Gate
Ypres
Flanders Fields

A walk along the town walls of Ypres takes you through many layers of European history. The walls have been attacked, destroyed and rebuilt many times, leaving behind traces from every period. You pass the remains of Burgundian towers, French bastions and a couple of concrete pill boxes built by the British. Begin at the Menin Gate and follow the walls around until you come to the station.

252 PALINGBEEK
De Palingbeek
Palingbeekstraat 18
Ypres
Flanders Fields
+32 (0)57 20 56 72
www.depalingbeek.be

Beginning at the restaurant De Palingbeek, you can follow forest trails that lead past the remains of a lost canal as well two small cemeteries hidden deep in the forest. Follow the walking route numbers: 15, 16, 17, 22, 23, 24, 25, 16 and 15.

253 HILL 60 TO CATERPILLAR CEMETERY

Zillebeke
Flanders Fields

One of the most interesting walks in Flanders Fields takes you to Hill 60 where an enormous mine went off on 17 April 1917. Starting at De Palingbeek restaurant (where there is a large car park), you follow a trail through the woods next to an old canal. You finally come to Caterpillar Crater where a mine went off on 7 June 1917. A bridge takes you across the railway line to Hill 60 where you can wander across a war-scarred landscape. Follow the numbers: 28, 27, 12, 13, 15, 26 and 27.

254 KEMMELBERG

Kemmelbergweg
Kemmel
Flanders Fields

The Kemmelberg is just 156 metres high. But that makes it the highest hill in the region. You can walk around the hill on forest trails with striking views across the Heuvelland landscape. This hill was the scene of horrendous battles throughout the First World War, but the woods have grown back, leaving few traces of the war apart from a French military cemetery.

255 CRATERS AND MINES WALK

Wijtschate
Flanders Fields

A signposted walk takes you through the rolling fields near Wijtschate where a series of huge mines were detonated in 1917. The walk, which begins in Wijtschate, follows quiet country lanes past crater holes and small military cemeteries where many Irish soldiers are buried. Follow the small hexagonal signs marked: *Kraters en Mijnen wandelroute.*

The 5
ODDEST PLACE NAMES

256 **HILL 60**
Zillebeke
Flanders Fields

Hill 60 is a strange scarred landscape dotted with concrete bunkers and shell holes. It is not a natural hill at all, but an artificial spoil heap created in the 19th century during the construction of a railway cutting on the line from Ypres to Comines. It was called the *Côte d'Amants*, the Lovers' Hill, but was renamed Hill 60 during the war. Thousands of soldiers died fighting for this 60-metre-high hill.

257 **WIPERS**
Ypres
Flanders Fields

Thousands of troops passed through Ypres during the First World War. But they found the French name too hard to pronounce, so they turned it into Wipers. Now Ypres is officially known by its old Dutch name Ieper.

258 **POP**
Poperinge
Flanders Fields

The small town of Poperinge was crowded with soldiers on leave during World War One. They drank Flemish beer in local cafés like the Café de l'Espérance and La Poupée, and watched films in barns. But the Flemish word Poperinge was too hard to pronounce, so the soldiers simplified it to Pop.

259 **PLUG STREET**
Ploegsteert
Flanders Fields

Ploegsteert is a small Belgian village near the French border. The nearby wood was the scene of fierce fighting during World War One. But the soldiers could not pronounce the Flemish name, so it became Plug Street.

260 **WHITE SHEET**
Wijtschate
Flanders Fields

The village of Wijtschate stands on the low ridge to the south of Ypres. It was attacked in June 1917 by soldiers who referred to it by the easier name of White Sheet.

The 5
BEST FILMS
on Flanders Fields

261 YPRES
www.britishpathe.com

A strange curiosity, this silent documentary was made in 1925 by the War Office in London. Filmed in former trenches, it recreates the Ypres battles with a cast that included some of the soldiers who had fought there. The seven reels can be downloaded on the British Pathé website.

262 BENEATH HILL 60
www.beneathhill60.com.au

This low-budget Australian war movie filmed in 2009 tells the extraordinary story of the miners who tunnelled below Hill 60 near Ypres. Filmed in Australia in claustrophobic shafts, it records the terrifying secret war waged below the Flemish countryside as 19 secret mines were buried below the Messines Ridge. The one below Hill 60 exploded on 7 June 1917 to create the huge Caterpillar Crater that can still be seen in Palingbeek woods.

263 ALL QUIET ON THE WESTERN FRONT

Made in the United States in 1930, this film was based on Erich Maria Remarque's anti-war novel. The footage and sound have deteriorated over the years, yet it remains a classic war film made with former soldiers among the cast and an ending that no one ever forgets.

264 JOYEUX NOËL

The French director Christian Carion based his 2005 film Joyeux Noël on the extraordinary Christmas Truce in December 1914 when soldiers briefly stopped fighting in a small area of trenches near Ploegsteert. Filmed in French, English and German, it lingered on the strange moment when soldiers began singing carols in the snowy trenches.

265 IN FLANDERS FIELDS

www.invlaamse velden.be

The Belgian director Jan Matthys filmed the epic 10-part TV series *In Vlaamse Velden* in 2013. It tells the story of a Ghent family caught up in the chaos of the First World War.

The 5 most
STRIKING ART WORKS

266 **THE GRIEVING PARENTS**
Houtlandstraat
Vladslo
Flanders Fields

The German cemetery at Vladslo is a quiet place in the countryside where few people ever go. It contains graves of 25,638 soldiers who died in this region of Belgium, including the son of the German sculptor Käthe Kollwitz.

267 **FALLS THE SHADOW**
Berten Pilstraat 5
Zonnebeke
Flanders Fields
+32 (0)51 77 04 41
www.passchendaele.be

The New Zealand sculptor Helen Pollock created a stunning new installation for the Passchendaele Memorial Museum in 2009. She used clay from the fields near Passchendaele to mould a series of arms reaching towards the sky.

268 **AUSTRALIAN MEMORIAL PLAQUES**
Passendaleplaats
Passendale
Flanders Fields

Ross J. Bastiaan is a dentist and amateur historian who creates bronze memorial plaques of Australian battlefields across the world. He has worked obsessively since 1990 to create more than 120 of these plaques, which incorporate detailed relief maps and simple accounts of the battles.

269 THE GRIEVING SOLDIERS

Klerkenstraat
Langemark
Flanders Fields

Four bronze figures of soldiers mourning a dead friend stand at the far end of Langemark Cemetery. They were carved by the Munich sculptor Emil Krieger in 1956 when this cemetery was expanded. Krieger based the figures on an old photograph of German soldiers taken in France in 1918.

270 COMING WORLD REMEMBER ME

Palingbeek estate
Zonnebeke
Flanders Fields
*www.comingworld
rememberme.be*

Some 600,000 small clay figures are to be created to represent soldiers killed in the Ypres area. Many have already been moulded by school students on visits to the battlefields. The 600,000 figures will finally form a land art installation at Palingbeek estate due to be unveiled on 11 November 2018.

267 FALLS THE SHADOW

The 5 most unusual
WAR MEMORIALS

271 ISLAND OF IRELAND PEACE PARK

Armentierssteenweg
Mesen
Flanders Fields

Here is one of the most extraordinary war monuments in Flanders Fields. It commemorates Protestant and Catholic soldiers who fought alongside one another in the battle to secure the Messines Ridge. The site is dominated by a replica Irish stone tower built by Irish workers in 1998 using stones from destroyed British army barracks and a former workhouse. The tower was unveiled on 11 November 1998 by the British queen and the Irish president in a symbolic act of reconciliation.

272 WELSH MEMORIAL

Hagebos
Flanders Fields

A simple Welsh cromlech made with grey flagstones stands in a field on the road from Ypres to Langemark. It was put up in 2014 by local people who felt there should be a memorial to Welsh soldiers killed in Flanders. It stands in a field close to the spot where the poet Hedd Wyn was killed.

271 ISLAND OF IRELAND PEACE PARK

274 BROODING SOLDIER

273 LA CARREFOUR DES ROSES

Langemarkseweg
Boezinge
Flanders Fields

A massive dolmen stands next to a crossroads on the road from Boezinge to Langemark. The eight huge stones were brought here from Brittany, along with a stone calvary from the village of Plouagat, to commemorate soldiers from the region who died when poison gas drifted across the trenches near here in April 1914.

274 BROODING SOLDIER

Zonnebekestraat
Sint-Julien
Flanders Fields

Here is one of the impressive war memorials in Flanders Fields. It was designed by the architect Chapman Clemsha in memory of 2,000 Canadian soldiers killed in the first gas attack in April 1915. The massive column carved from a single piece of granite is surmounted by a solemn figure of a grieving soldier.

275 CHRISTMAS TRUCE CROSS

Chemin du Mont
de la Hutte
Ploegsteert
Flanders Fields

A strange wooden cross stands next to a quiet country road near Prowse Point Military Cemetery. It was put up a few years ago to commemorate the Christmas Truce in 1914 when German and British soldiers left the trenches to sing songs, exchange gifts and play a friendly game of football in No Man's Land. The match took place in a field somewhere near the cross. It has become a shrine where people leave footballs, team strips and even souvenir mugs.

The 5 best
BOOKS TO READ
about Flanders Fields

---

276 ALL QUIET ON THE WESTERN FRONT

The German writer Erich Maria Remarque spent just six weeks in the trenches. He arrived on 12 June and was evacuated on 31 July after being hit by shell fragments during the Battle of Passchendaele. Yet his 1929 book *All Quiet on the Western Front* is one of the great anti-war novels. It was later made into a film and banned by Hitler as degenerate.

277 SOME DESPERATE GLORY

Edwin Campion Vaughan kept a diary during the war that records his experiences during the Battle of Passchendale in 1917. The diary was found after his death in 1931, but kept hidden in a cupboard for 40 years. It was finally published in 1981 under the title *Some Desperate Glory, The Diary of a Young Officer, 1917*. It was described by one critic as 'one of the five best books on war'.

278 THE WET FLANDERS PLAIN

The British writer Henry Williamson wrote several books based on his experiences of the First World War. *The Wet Flanders Plain* is a strangely beautiful travel book written after he returned to the battlefields of Flanders in 1928. It was published in the same year as *Goodbye to All That* and *All Quiet on the Western Front*. Williamson also wrote about the war in his 15-volume *A Chronicle of Ancient Sunlight*.

279 BEFORE ENDEAVOURS FADE

Rose Coombs was a researcher at the Imperial War Museum in London who published a guide to the battlefields of the Somme and Flanders in 1977. She was especially fond of the Ramparts Cemetery in Ypres where her ashes were scattered in 1991. The book is amazingly still in print in an updated version with new photographs.

280 TESTAMENT OF YOUTH

First published in 1933, Vera Brittain's haunting chronicle of war tells of four men she knew who were killed in the war, including her brother and fiancé. She also writes of her experience as a nurse in 1917 when she helped to look after British and German soldiers wounded in the Battle of Passchendaele.

PALINGBEEK NATURE RESERVE

20 PLACES TO DISCOVER THE YPRES REGION

The 5 best VIEWS in Flanders Fields —————— 144

The 5 most inspiring CASTLES —————— 147

The 5 best SMALL MUSEUMS
in Flanders Fields —————— 149

The 5 most interesting MUSEUMS IN
FRENCH FLANDERS —————— 152

The 5 best
VIEWS
in Flanders Fields

---

281 YPRES BELFRY

Grote Markt 34
Ypres
+32 (0)57 23 92 20
www.inflandersfields.be

You can climb up to the top of the reconstructed mediaeval Belfry for a spectacular view of the old town and the Ypres Salient. It is a steep climb of 231 steps, beginning with a narrow spiral staircase and ending with a narrow metal gangway suspended in the bell tower. But the view is worth the effort.

282 LONE TREE CEMETERY

Kruisstraat
Wijtschate
Flanders Fields

This small cemetery is located on high ground captured from the Germans in 1917. Standing here, you get a sweeping view of the countryside where hundreds of Irish soldiers died in the summer of 1917. The view takes in the wooded hill Kemmelberg and the church spires in Mesen and Wijtschate.

283 PALINGBEEK CENTRE

Palingbeekstraat 18
Ypres
Flanders Fields
+32 (0)57 20 56 72
www.depalingbeek.be

The Palingbeek nature centre stands on the ridge south of Ypres where German trenches once snaked across the land. You get a striking view from the road looking across open fields to the reconstructed mediaeval spires of Ypres in the distance.

284 KEMMELBERG BELVEDERE

Kemmelbergweg
Kemmel
Flanders Fields

The belvedere at the top of the Kemmelberg has been a tourist attraction since the 19th century. The original building was destroyed in the First World War, but rebuilt in the 1920s. It was a rather run-down attraction until recently when a new owner restored the building. You can climb to the top for a sweeping view of the battlefields.

285 RODEBERG CHAIR LIFT

Rodebergstraat 75
Westouter
Flanders Fields
+32 (0)57 44 60 35

An old-fashioned chair lift runs up a hill called Rodeberg. Built by an Austrian firm, it takes you above a vineyard planted on the sunny slopes of the Rodeberg. Some people say it's just like the Alps.

284 KEMMELBERG BELVEDERE

288 PALINGBEEK NATURE CENTRE

286 ELZENWALLE

The 5 most inspiring
C A S T L E S

---

286 **ELZENWALLE**
Kemmelseweg 72
Voormezele
Flanders Fields

Kasteel Elzenwalle is a strange modern castle built in 1921 on the foundations of an 18th century building shelled to bits in the war. The Art Nouveau architect Ernest Blerot rebuilt the castle using fragments of the old building and wood from shattered trees on the estate. The most striking feature is a reinforced concrete dome that locals say looks like a German Pickelhaube helmet.

287 **VLAMERTINGE**
Hospitaalstraat 28
Vlamertinge
Flanders Fields

This beautiful 19th century Flemish Renaissance style castle is surrounded by romantic gardens. Located to the west of Ypres, it was occupied by the British army during the war. A small monument near the castle gates has the words of Edmund Blunden's poem *Vlamertinghe: Passing the Chateau, July 1917*. He wrote the poem while based here in July 1917, while soldiers prepared for the start of the Battle of Passchendaele.

288 ELVERDINGE

Vlamertingse-
straat 83
Elverdinge
Flanders Fields

Located just a few kilometres west of the front line, the beautiful rococo castle on the edge of Elverdinge village was occupied by the British army during World War One. The village church nearby was destroyed in 1915 and the castle was gutted by a fire in 1918, possibly caused by careless British troops. After the war it was rebuilt in its old style.

289 BEAUVOORDE

Wulveringem-
straat 10
Veurne
Flanders Fields
+32 (0)58 29 92 29
www.beauvoorde.be

This is a beautiful ancient castle surrounded by apple orchards. It looks like a 17th century Flemish castle with step gables and turrets, but it is really a romantic fantasy built in the 19th century by a local aristocrat. The rooms are filled with 17th century furniture to complete the illusion. The nearby village has some restaurants where you can eat well, like the rustic *'t Potje Paté*.

290 DE LOVIE

Krombeekseweg 82
Poperinge
Flanders Fields

This 19th century castle near Poperinge survived the war with little damage. It now serves as a support centre for handicapped people. It will host two innovative art installations in 2015 linked to the first German gas attack of 22 April 1915. The British artist Simon Chatterton's *Sea of Green* sets out to evoke the gas attack using sound, film and pyrotechnics, while Peter de Cupere's *The Smell of War* will immerse the castle in the smells of war.

The 5 best
SMALL MUSEUMS
in Flanders Fields

291 HOP MUSEUM

Gasthuisstraat 71
Poperinge
Flanders Fields
+32 (0)57 33 79 22
www.hopmuseum.be

You might ask if a hop museum can be all that interesting. But this place is fascinating. It occupies a huge old warehouse where hops were once stored. The museum spreads over four floors, with rooms filled with ancient equipment, old photographs and beer posters.

292 SCHOOL MUSEUM

Gustave De Stuers-
straat 6A
Ypres
Flanders Fields
+32 (0)57 23 92 20
www.toerismeieper.be

Located in a Neo-Romanesque church, the School Museum (Onderwijsmuseum) doesn't sound too tempting. But it is a strangely captivating place with an extensive collection of old school books, globes, educational posters and schoolbags. One section charts the destruction of Ypres' schools in 1914-18 and the fate of the children forced to flee to France. You can also peer inside two old classrooms.

291 **HOP MUSEUM**

293 YPRES CITY MUSEUM

Ieperleestraat 31
Ypres
Flanders Fields
+32 (0)57 23 92 20
www.toerismeieper.be

The town of Ypres was flattened in the First World War, but a 16th-century almshouse called Sint-Jangodshuis partly survived. It is now occupied by the city museum, which has a small collection of old maps, photographs and archaeological finds, along with paintings by the Ypres artist Louis De Hem. Entry is free if you have bought a ticket to In Flanders Fields Museum.

294 KÄTHE KOLLWITZ MUSEUM

Sint-Maartens-
plein 15B
Koekelare
Flanders Fields
+32 (0)51 61 04 94
www.koekelare.be

A small but fascinating museum is located in a recently restored malting tower attached to an old brewery. It tells the story of Pieter Kollwitz, one of the many students who joined the German army at the beginning of the war and died in the 'Massacre of the Innocents' on 23-24 October 1914. His mother Käthe Kollwitz created the two figures of grieving parents in Vladslo Cemetery. The museum has 70 original drawings by Kollwitz on the themes of death and war.

295 LANGE MAX MUSEUM

Clevenstraat 2
Koekelare
Flanders Fields
+32 (0)475 58 50 51
www.langemax.be

This small museum does not get many visitors. But that makes it more special. Located in an old farm that was used as a German officers' mess, it tells the story of the German occupation in this region of Belgium. The main attraction lies in the old barn where an exhibition is devoted to a massive German gun positioned near here that could fire a shell as far as Dunkirk.

The 5 most interesting
MUSEUMS
IN FRENCH FLANDERS

296 FRAC

503 Rue des Bancs de
Flandres
Dunkerque
French Flanders
(France)
+33 (0)3 28 65 84 20
www.fracnpdc.fr

This spectacular new contemporary art museum is located in the heart of Dunkirk's port area. Designed by architects Anne Lacaton and Jean-Philippe Vassal, the glass building stands next to an old ship building yard. The centre organises temporary exhibitions based on its collection of contemporary art. But it is worth visiting simply for the spectacular architecture and the view of the port from the top floor.

297 LOUVRE LENS

99 Rue Paul Bert
Lens
French Flanders
(France)
+33 (0)3 21 18 62 62
www.louvrelens.fr

The Japanese architects Sanaa have designed a sleek minimalist museum on the site of an old slag heap near the town of Lens in northern France. The interior is a single vast hangar enclosed by aluminium walls that create dream-like reflections of the visitors and the art. Displayed here are works from the Louvre's collection, including Delacroix's Liberty Leading the People.

298 LAAC

Pont Lucien Lefol
Dunkerque
French Flanders
(France)
+33 (0)3 28 29 56 00
*www.musees-
dunkerque.eu*

Dunkirk's contemporary art museum occupies a 1982 building near the beach where British troops were evacuated in 1940. Surrounded by a sculpture garden, it exhibits modern art from its extensive collection and occasionally organises quirky exhibitions.

299 MUSÉE DE FLANDRE

26 Grand'Place
Cassel
French Flanders
(France)
+33 (0)3 59 73 45 60
*www.museedeflandre.
cg59.fr*

It took 13 years to restore this old museum in northern France, but it was worth the wait. The 16th century mansion has been sensitively renovated to create a sumptuous setting for an interesting local collection of Flemish furniture and paintings.

300 LA PISCINE

23 Rue de
l'Espérence
Roubaix
French Flanders
(France)
+33 (0)3 20 69 23 60
*www.roubaix-
lapiscine.com*

This is a stunning art museum located in a former Art Deco swimming pool dating from 1932. The collection includes sculptures, decorative art and paintings. But the extraordinary building is the main attraction. Some objects are displayed in the restored changing cubicles.

BLANKENBERGE BEACH

70 PLACES TO GO AT THE BELGIAN COAST

The 5 most original BEACH TOWNS ———— 158

The 5 best SMALL AND UNUSUAL
MUSEUMS at the coast ———— 161

The 5 best WALKS IN THE DUNES ———— 163

The 5 most REMARKABLE BUILDINGS
at the coast ———— 165

The 5 most ATTRACTIVE
NEIGHBOURHOODS ———— 167

The 5 most QUIET PLACES on the coast ———— 169

The 5 best CYCLE TRIPS at the coast ———— 171

The 5 best FREE THINGS TO DO
at the coast ———— 173

The 5 STRANGEST SCULPTURES
on the coast ———————————————— 175

The 5 strangest places along
the COAST TRAM ROUTE ———————— 177 ·

The 5 best CONTEMPORARY
GALLERIES ———————————————— 179

The 5 best places for CULTURE
on the coast ———————————————— 181

The 5 best VIEWS *at the coast* —————— 184

The 5 best MINI GOLF COURSES ————— 186

The 5 most original
BEACH TOWNS

---

301 NIEUWPOORT
TOURIST OFFICE:
Marktplein 7
Nieuwpoort
Belgian Coast
+32 (0)58 22 44 44
www.nieuwpoort.be

No one went to Nieuwpoort in the past, but now it is one of the coolest places on the Belgian coast with some excellent restaurants and stylish B&Bs. The old town is an interesting place to wander, while the huge marina is packed with sailing boats.

302 OSTEND
TOURIST OFFICE:
Monacoplein 2-9
Ostend
Belgian Coast
+32 (0)59 70 11 99
www.visitoostende.be

Ostend has stopped calling itself "The Queen of the Belgian Resorts," yet this faded seaside town still has a genteel charm as well as a vibrant night life. You find some good fish restaurants in the old town, as well as excellent museums, cafés and shops.

303 DE HAAN
TOURIST OFFICE:
Tramstation
De Haan
Belgian Coast
+32 (0)59 24 21 34
www.visitdehaan.be

De Haan is a charming resort that has hardly changed since it was laid out in a dreamy German romantic style in the 19th century. The strict planning laws laid down at the time have prevented the construction of modern apartment buildings, and you still find small family-run hotels, unique B&Bs and friendly restaurants.

304 **BLANKENBERGE**

305 **KNOKKE**

305 **KNOKKE**

304 BLANKENBERGE

TOURIST OFFICE:
Koning Leopold III-
Plein
Blankenberge
Belgian Coast
+32 (0)50 41 22 27
www.blankenberge.be

Blankenberge is a busy resort with an impressive concrete pier and the occasional lovely Art Nouveau villa lurking among the modern apartment buildings. It isn't particularly pretty, but it has a certain old-fashioned Belgian charm. You can stay in an Art Nouveau B&B, eat a sticky waffle on the promenade and sit at the end of the pier with a beer. It might just turn out to be your favourite place on the coast.

305 KNOKKE

TOURIST OFFICE:
Zeedijk 660
Knokke
Belgian Coast
+32 (0)50 63 03 80
www.knokke-heist.info

Knokke is a glamorous and slightly haughty resort where rich northern Europeans spend their weekends. Developed in the 19th century by the Lippens family, it tries to remain exclusive by banning picnic boxes, kites and parties on the beach. The town centre is dominated by high fashion and exclusive brands which make it rather soulless. But it has attractive quarters where residents drive around in quaint golf buggies.

The 5 best
SMALL AND UNUSUAL
MUSEUMS *at the coast*

306 ENSOR HOUSE
Vlaanderenstraat 27
Ostend
Belgian Coast
+32 (0)59 80 53 35
www.muzee.be

This bizarre museum devoted to the eccentric Ostend artist James Ensor is located above a former souvenir shop run by his aunt and uncle. Ensor lived here from 1917 until his death in 1945. The ground floor is crammed with an odd collection of shells, masks and other seaside souvenirs.

307 STADSMUSEUM OOSTENDE
Langestraat 69
Ostend
Belgian Coast
+32 (0)59 51 67 21
www.oostende.be/
stadsmuseum

The fascinating Ostend city museum is located in the former summer residence of the Belgian royal family. The grand, slightly shabby rooms are filled with an eclectic collection of Ostend curiosities gathered by the local history society, including ship models, sea charts, souvenirs and ferry timetables.

308 KUSTHISTORIES
Joseph Casselaan 1
Middelkerke
Belgian Coast
+32 (0)59 30 03 68
www.kusthistories.be

This is a small, quirky museum in the resort of Middelkerke with a nostalgic collection of seaside mementoes. You see old posters, postcards and beach toys, along with battered suitcases, café signs, hotel crockery and bathing costumes.

309 BELLE EPOQUE CENTRUM

Elisabethstraat 24
Blankenberge
Belgian Coast
+32 (0)50 42 87 41
www.belle.epoque.
blankenberge.be

Here is one of the most charming museums on the coast. Located in three restored Belle Epoque houses, it is filled with relics from the time when Blankenberge was the most elegant resort on the North Sea. You can enter a living room furnished in period style, listen to music hall songs and step out onto an astonishing roof terrace with a replica Gaudi bench made using ceramic tiles salvaged from demolished seaside houses.

310 NAVIGO

Pastoor Schmitz-
straat 5
Oostduinkerke
Belgian Coast
+32 (0)58 51 24 68
www.navigomuseum.be

This is a captivating fishing museum filled with the sound of screeching gulls. It displays a vast collection of maritime relics including films, photographs and paintings. The museum also has a fisherman's cottage, a fishing boat and a small aquarium.

306 ENSOR HOUSE

The 5 best
WALKS IN THE DUNES

_____

311 DE PANNE TO BRAY-DUNES

The Belgian Coast often looks like an unbroken line of apartment buildings, but there are still areas of wild dunes where you can wander along peaceful trails. One of the wildest walks takes you through the dunes between De Panne and the French beach town of Bray-Dunes, where Belgians go to drink a glass of a strange alcoholic drink called _picon_.

312 TER YDE NATURE RESERVE

A wild area of dunes stretches for several kilometres just behind Oostduinkerke. Here you can wander along marked trails and possibly spot rare breeding birds like the Tawny Pipit as well as a herd of Shetland ponies brought here to keep the grass from growing wild.

313 DE HAAN

The dunes between De Haan and Wenduine were planted with pine trees in the 19th century. You can follow a meandering trail through the woods for an hour or so, and then return to De Haan along a beach where Belgians ride horses in the winter.

314 **BAAI VAN HEIST**

Not many people know about the small nature reserve that lies to the west of Heist. You can wander through a small area of wild dunes and return to Heist along the empty beach. A footbridge takes you across the main road to another nature reserve where you can sometimes spot rare birds.

315 **HET ZWIN**

The Zwin is a wild area of marshland and dunes lying to the east of Knokke. You can set off on foot on marked trails that lead eventually to the small Dutch beach town of Cadzand.

312 TER YDE NATURE RESERVE

The 5 most
REMARKABLE BUILDINGS
at the coast

---

316 VILLA LES ZÉPHYRS

Henri Jasparlaan 173
Westende
Belgian Coast
+32 (0)59 91 28
www.kusthistories.be

Middelkerke may not seem particularly interesting, but it has one architectural gem. The strange Villa Les Zéphyrs was built in 1922 as a modern seaside house for a Ghent doctor's family. It now looks a bit lost among the apartment buildings, but it still has a beautiful Art Nouveau interior created by Henry van de Velde in 1898 (for a different house). It can be visited with the same ticket as the Kusthistories museum.

317 DE HAAN VILLAS

Rembrandtlaan 10-17
De Haan
Belgian Coast

Some of the loveliest houses in De Haan were built by the Ghent architect Valentin Vaerwyck in 1925-27 on the Rembrandtlaan. Here he created a romantic architectural style featuring whitewashed brick, steep red tiled roofs and bright green-and-white shutters. Some of the houses have façade stones that refer to their name, like the one on Villa Roodkapje (Little Red Riding Hood Villa), which looks like a page from a children's story book.

318 THE BLACK HOUSE
Dumortierlaan 8
Knokke
Belgian Coast

The architect Huib Hoste built a daring modernist house in 1924 for a local doctor. The sleek black façade was inspired by the Dutch architecture of De Stijl movement. The house lay empty for many years, until a gallery owner rescued it from ruin.

319 GRAND HÔTEL BELLEVUE
Zeedijk 300
Westende
Belgian Coast

This was one of the most luxurious hotels on the Belgian coast when it opened in 1911. Designed by Octave Van Rysselberghe, it was constructed in a modern style using reinforced concrete. The town was shelled to bits in the First World War, but the hotel remained standing. The building was recently renovated and turned into apartments.

320 DE LICHTLIJN BRIDGE
Elizabethlaan
Knokke
Belgian Coast

The engineer Laurent Ney designed a sensual curved bridge called *De Lichtlijn*, or the Light Line, in 2008. It carries cyclists and pedestrians across the busy coast road in a gorgeous curving sweep.

The 5 most
ATTRACTIVE
NEIGHBOURHOODS

---

321 DUMONT QUARTER

Hoge Duinenlaan
De Panne
Belgian Coast

A cluster of old beach houses lies hidden in the dunes to the south of De Panne. The houses were built by the Brussels architects Albert Dumont and Georges Hobé in a distinctive rustic style inspired by English cottages. Hobé built his own beach house on Hoge Duinenlaan on top of the highest dune.

322 SÉNÉGALAIS QUARTER

Bad Schallerbach-
plein
Koksijde
Belgian Coast

The architect Gaston Lejeune built this romantic district of holiday villas for wealthy Belgian industrialists in 1908. Six years after they were finished, these quaint Anglo-Norman style houses were occupied by French colonial troops defending the town of Nieuwpoort. The quarter was later named after the Senegalese troops who briefly stayed there.

323 SINT ROCHUS QUARTER

Elisabethstraat
Blankenberge
Belgian Coast

The seaside town of Blankenberge has some of the finest Art Nouveau houses on the coast. Clustered around the Sint-Rochuskerk, these romantic town houses are decorated with ironwork, balconies and loggias with curious tile pictures.

324 **DE CONCESSIE**

De Haan
Belgian Coast

Get off the tram at De Haan to walk along the quiet meandering lanes where the German architect Joseph Stübben designed a model town in 1910. Known as De Concessie, it is a deeply romantic quarter where you find quaint white houses with steep red roofs that look as if they belong in a German fairy tale.

325 **HET ZOUTE**

Knokke
Belgian Coast

The most exclusive quarter on the Belgian coast lies in the dunes to the east of Knokke. Designed by the planner who created De Haan, this is a district of meandering lanes and romantic whitewashed villas. It has become a favourite retreat for élite industrialists and bankers, giving it something of the air of the Hamptons or Saint-Tropez.

324 DE HAAN

The 5
QUIET PLACES
on the coast

326 OSTEND EAST BEACH
Halvemaandijk
Ostend
Belgian Coast

Take the ferry across Ostend harbour and follow signs to Fort Napoleon. A path leads through the dunes to a quiet stretch of beach where almost no one goes, not even in the summer.

327 LOUISE-MARIE CHAPEL
Sint-Petrus-en-Paulusplein
Ostend
Belgian Coast

Not many people look inside Ostend's dark neo-Gothic church built in 1905. But it contains a beautiful secret chapel behind the altar with a sad marble monument dedicated to Queen Louise-Marie. She died in Ostend at the age of 38 in a house that is now the city museum. The statue shows the dying queen gazing up at an angel.

328 OUR LADY OF THE DUNES CHURCH
Dorpstraat
Ostend
Belgian Coast

James Ensor was fond of this curious little church in the dunes lit by hundreds of tiny red candles. It was built in the 17th century on the site of a much older church destroyed during the Siege of Ostend. It has a quaint altar made from sea shells, along with dusty ship models, a painting of the Spanish Armada and old photographs of shipwrecks.

329 UITKERKSE POLDER

Kuiperscheeweg 20
Blankenberge
Belgian Coast
+32 (0)50 42 90 40
www.uitkerkse-
polder.be

You only need to cycle out of Blankenberge for ten minutes to reach this empty flat polder landscape dotted with a few whitewashed farmhouses. Several trails lead across the wild, waterlogged meadows where you can sometimes see wintering birds like teal and widgeon.

330 ZUYDCOOTE

Rue des
Valenciennes
Zuydcoote
French Flanders
(France)

Here is a quiet undisturbed beach in northern France just a few kilometres from the Belgian border. It can be busy in the summer, but at other times it is a wonderful wild spot where the only sound is the wind blowing through the dunes.

326 OSTEND FORT NAPOLEON

The best
CYCLE TRIPS
at the coast

331 NIEUWPOORT TO WESTENDE

Begin by crossing the River Yser at the impressive Albert I Monument and follow the quiet route across fields to reach Lombardsijde. The return route passes through the quiet nature reserve De IJzermonding where birds fly over salt marshes and seal are sometimes washed ashore. The tour ends with a trip across the river on a jaunty red free ferry. Follow the cycle route signs numbered 82, 67, 7, 8, 9, 12, 81 and 82.

332 OSTEND TO MIDDELKERKE

A beautiful windswept stretch of coastal cycle path runs for 11km from Ostend to Middelkerke. The route takes you past the Wellington racecourse and the church of Our Lady of the Dunes. You can return to Ostend along quiet country roads and canal towpaths, ending with a stretch along an old railway line called Spoor 62 that once carried trains from Paris to Ostend. Follow numbers: 4, 52, 80, 14, 15, 16, 17, 18, 53, 20, 11, 2, 1 and 4.

333 BLANKENBERGE TO BRUGES

It doesn't take much more than an hour to cycle from Blankenberge to Bruges along quiet roads with little traffic. From the station in Blankenberge, cycle next to the railway line and then cross the flat polders until you see the spires of Bruges. For the return journey, you can cross the Uitkerkse Polder where migrating birds gather. Follow numbers: 32, 33, 27, 40, 41, 62, 64, 58, 61, 19, 15, 10, 30 and 31.

334 KNOKKE TO CADZAND

One of the most interesting routes takes you out of Knokke to Het Zwin nature reserve where you can cycle along the sea dike all the way to the Dutch town of Cadzand. You can then return to Knokke through the old fortress town of Retranchement, and along old canals that cross the flat polders. Follow numbers: 42, 45, 29, 32, 33, 30, 50, 51, 46, 45 and 42.

335 KOKSIJDE TO VEURNE

You can cycle inland from Koksijde to Veurne, an attractive old town with several good cafés, and then return through De Panne. Follow numbers 65, 66, 6, 5 and 60 to get to Veurne.

The 5 best

FREE THINGS TO DO

at the coast

---

336 NIEUWPOORT FERRY

Paul Orban-
promenade
Nieuwpoort
Belgian Coast

It's fun to hop on the free ferry that was introduced in 2011 to take people across the Yser estuary. It was painted by Roger Raveel and was christened *Het Rode Vierkant op Zee*, the Red Square at Sea. It leaves from the Westerstaketsel jetty and drops you off a few minutes later on the edge of a windswept nature reserve. You can then hike along the beach to Westende and take the tram back to Nieuwpoort.

337 KIJKHUT DE ZEEHOND

De IJzermonding
Nieuwpoort
Belgian Coast

Here is a place where you can escape the crowds. This birdwatching hide was built in the IJzermonding nature reserve near the estuary of the Yser in 2007. It has benches where you sit in the dark watching rare birds gather along the muddy tidal riverbank. Sometimes you hear nothing but the screeching of gulls.

338 SUMMER CONCERTS

www.dekust.be/festivals

Every Belgian resort organises music festivals and concerts in the summer. Look out for posters in tourist offices and local bars. Sometimes you have to buy a ticket. But often the concerts are free events where you just turn up on the day and find a place to sit down.

339 OSTEND FERRY

Visserskaai
Ostend
Belgian Coast

A small free ferry leaves regularly from the Aquarium in Ostend to take people and bicycles across the harbour to the old docks. You can then follow signs to Fort Napoleon or head down to the quiet beach just behind the dunes.

340 PARKING

www.dehaan.be

Belgians as a rule do not like to pay for parking, even though it only costs a few euro. They prefer to hunt for a parking place along the coast road. Or they drive to De Haan which is the only town on the coast where you can park for free (usually for two hours if you display a blue disc). But maybe it is just better to put some coins in the machine.

The 5
STRANGEST SCULPTURES
on the coast

341 **CHRISTOPHORUS**
Dynastielaan
De Panne
Belgian Coast

The coastline is dotted with 26 contemporary sculptures that were originally commissioned for the Beaufort art festivals. You occasionally come across a strange work hidden in the dunes, like Gerhard Lentink's giant wooden torso near De Panne. Created for the first Beaufort festival in 2003, the wooden structure has weathered over the years to a strange grey tint.

342 **LE VENT SOUFFLE OU IL VEUT**
Krommehoek
Nieuwpoort
Belgian Beach

Daniel Buren's curious art installation stands in a remote spot on Nieuwpoort harbour. It features one hundred flagpoles with striped windsocks at the top that turn in the wind. With a title meaning 'The Wind Blows Wherever it Pleases', the installation was made for Beaufort's 2003 art festival.

343 ROSE DES VENTS II

Driehoeksplein
Knokke
Belgian Coast

Wim Delvoye is a Belgian artist who likes to shock. He has created tattooed pigs, an excrement machine and erotic stained glass windows. Now he has shocked the more sensitive residents of Knokke with this statue of a male angel pissing in the wind.

344 ROCK STRANGERS

Zeeheldenplein
Ostend
Belgian Coast

The Belgian artist Arne Quinze likes to create mysterious urban sculptures in unexpected locations. Sometimes they do not last very long. But the enormous red metal sculptures called Rock Strangers are a permanent fixture on the promenade in Ostend.

345 BABIES

Zeedijk 150
Blankenberge
Belgian Coast

One of the oddest art installations can be spotted in Blankenberge, where two enormous black babies climb up the façade of the casino while a third stands on top looking out to sea. The Czech artist David Cerny created these three babies for the 2006 art festival Beaufort 02. They were originally displayed on the promenade, but ended up on Blankenberge's hideous modern casino.

The 5 strangest places along the
COAST TRAM ROUTE

---

346 NORMANDIE

Koninklijke Baan 1
Koksijde
Belgian Coast

You pass some strange and beautiful places on the coast tram. But possibly the strangest building comes just outside Koksijde where you glimpse a bizarre restaurant in the dunes in the shape of the French transatlantic liner Normandie. Built in concrete in 1935, it has two funnels, a deck and several portholes.

347 ALBERT I MONUMENT

Sluizen
Nieuwpoort
Belgian Coast

You cannot miss the huge circular brick monument outside Nieuwpoort on the banks of the River Yser. It was put up in 1938 in honour of King Albert I and the Belgian lock-keepers who died opening the sluices in 1914 to stop the German advance.

348 HEIST LIGHTHOUSE

Elizabethlaan
Heist
Belgian Coast

You see several lighthouses as the tram rattles along the coast, but the strangest stands in a field near Zeebrugge, a long way from the sea. The reinforced concrete tower was built by the Grondel brothers in 1907 in a style inspired by Art Nouveau.

349 LEEUWENBRUG SCULPTURES

Graaf de Smet de
Naeyerlaan
Ostend
Belgian Coast

Soon after leaving Ostend railway station, the tram crosses a series of bridges, including one called the *Leeuwenbrug*, or Lions' Bridge, which is decorated with strange sculptures of steam locomotives that seem to be emerging from the stone. The bridge was built in 1900 as part of Leopold II's ambitious plan to create a tram line along the 67-kilometre coastline.

350 DE HAAN TRAM STATION

Tramlijn Oost
De Haan
Belgian Coast

The tram pulls up in De Haan next to a beautiful Art Nouveau station built in 1888. It was designed by the Brussels architect G. Dhaeyer in a fanciful style with steep overhanging eaves, elegant carved wood and the French name Coq-sur-Mer in decorative letters.

346 NORMANDIE

The 5 best
CONTEMPORARY GALLERIES

351 GALERIE RONNY VAN DE VELDE

Zeedijk 759
Knokke
Belgian Coast
+32 (0)50 60 13 50
www.ronny
vandevelde.com

Several upmarket galleries representing Belgian and international artists have opened in Knokke. Most are located on the smart Zeedijk promenade facing the sea, including Ronny Van de Velde, an Antwerp gallery that deals in major artists like Marcel Duchamp, René Magritte and James Ensor.

352 GALERIE ZWART HUIS

Zeedijk 635
Knokke
Belgian Coast
www.galerie
zwarthuis.be

The Zwart Huis, or Black house still gives his name to Gerda Vander Kerken's gallery, even though she has moved out of the striking 1924 modernist house where she opened her gallery in 2001. She now has a gallery on the promenade where she displays exciting new work by Belgian artists, photographers, fashion designers and graphic artists.

353 GEUKENS & DE VIL

Zeedijk 735
Knokke
Belgian Coast
+32 (0)474 38 20 68
+32 (0)475 39 83 99
www.geukensdevil.com

Art historians Yasmine Geukens and Marie-Paule De Vil decided to open a gallery in Knokke in 1998. Here they display an inspiring range of contemporary artists in a modern space facing the sea. They have a second gallery in Antwerp where they focus on edgy experimental art.

354 ANDRÉ SIMOENS GALLERY

Kustlaan 130
Knokke
Belgian Coast
+32 (0)50 62 20 91
www.andresimoens
gallery.com

André Simoens opened a gallery in 1978 in a white complex close to the sea. He represents established Belgian artists such as Marie-Jo Lafontaine, Wim Delvoye and Raoul De Keyser. He also sells works by international photographers like Martin Parr and Hiroshi Sugimoto.

355 SAMUEL VANHOEGAERDEN GALLERY

Zeedijk 720
Knokke
Belgian Coast
+32 (0)477 51 09 89
www.svhgallery.be

Samuel van Hoegaerden is a young independent gallery owner who opens his seafront gallery at weekends. He displays works by established contemporary artists like Alexander Calder, Hans Hartung and Keith Haring. He also likes to promote the neglected Belgian artist Fred Eerdekens.

353 GEUKENS & DE VIL

352 GALERIE ZWART HUIS

The 5 best places for
CULTURE
on the coast

---

356 DE GROTE POST

Hendrik
Serruyslaan 18A
Ostend
Belgian Coast
+32 (0)59 33 90 00
www.degrotepost.be

Ostend's modernist post office closed down in 1999 and lay empty for many years until the city finally decided to turn it into a cultural centre. The architects B-Architecten have kept the modernist details such as the post office counters and phone booths, but added striking new elements. The building now has six performance spaces used for dance, theatre and rock concerts, as well as a café.

357 PAUL DELVAUX MUSEUM

Paul Delvauxlaan 42
Sint-Idesbald
Belgian Coast
+32 (0)58 52 12 29
www.delvaux
museum.com

The Belgian Surrealist artist Paul Delvaux lived most of his life in a whitewashed fisherman's cottage at the Belgian coast. The little house is now connected to a museum filled with Delvaux's haunting and disturbing paintings of empty train stations and melancholy nude women. We applaud the decision to install old wooden railway seats where you can sit looking at the paintings.

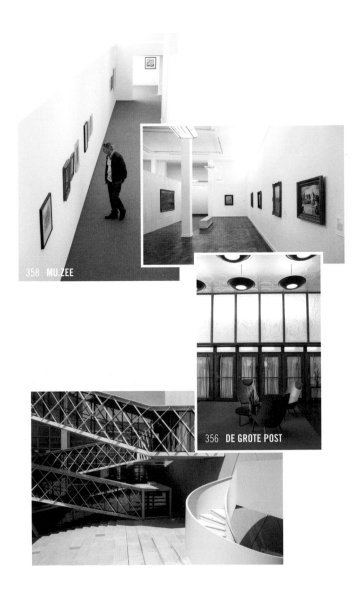

358 MU.ZEE

356 DE GROTE POST

358 MU.ZEE

Romestraat 11
Ostend
Belgian Coast
+32 (0)59 50 81 18
www.muzee.be

It's definitely worth spending some time in this beautiful modernist building once occupied by a cooperative department store. Displayed in calm white spaces, the collection includes works by Permeke, Ensor, Spilliaert and Broodthaers. But it also has some raw new art by Belgian artists like Jan Vercruysse and Jacqueline Mesmaeker.

359 PERMEKE MUSEUM

Gistelsteenweg 341
Jabbeke
Bruges region
+32 (0)50 81 12 88
www.permeke
museum.be
www.muzee.be

The Flemish Expressionist painter Constant Permeke lived in a solid modernist house he designed for himself near Bruges in 1930. The house has barely been touched since he died in 1952. You can wander through the rooms where he lived and look inside his sculpture studio. The house now contains a collection of 80 of his paintings, mostly rough earthy paintings of Flemish peasants and Ostend fishermen.

360 CINEMA RIO

Monicastraat 11
De Haan
Belgian Coast
+32 (0)477 26 27 68
cinemario.be

This is a nostalgic old neighbourhood cinema in the resort of De Haan. It was renovated in 1984, but has kept a certain period charm. The programme covers children's films, blockbusters and the occasional prize-winning movie from the Cannes or Berlin festivals.

The 5 best
V I E W S
at the coast

---

361 **SPIOENKOP**
Leopold II-laan
Wenduine
Belgian Coast

A little white observation post with a red roof was built in 1902 on top of the second-highest dune on the Belgian coast. You can see the spires of Bruges from up here when the weather is clear.

362 **BELGIUM PIER**
Zeedijk 261
Blankenberge
Belgian Coast
+32 (0)50 43 37 50
www.belgiumpier.be

The Art Deco pier in Blankenberge is a bit dilapidated, but it's still worth walking out to the end to look out across the North Sea. It is a stunning spot to stand when there is a storm at sea.

363 **ZEEBRUGGE PORT OBSERVATION PLATFORM**
Zweedse Kaai
Zeebrugge
Belgian Coast

The busy seaport of Zeebrugge has built a striking red metal cabin with a view of the modern docks. You can shelter inside on rainy days or climb up to the roof when the weather is good to watch massive Chinese car carriers and cruise ships slowly move through the port.

364 **OOSTERSTAKETSEL**

Loodswezenplein
Nieuwpoort
Belgian Coast

The beach can be a romantic place if you know where to look. One of the most appealing spots is at the far end of the long wooden jetty that juts out into the sea at Nieuwpoort-Bad. Constructed in the Yser estuary in 1865, it has survived two world wars. But the wooden structure is gradually rotting away, and sometimes has to be closed for long periods to carry out repairs.

365 **WEBCAMS**

www.dekust.be

Webcams have been installed at 19 points along the coast to provide live images of the beach. You can check the cameras before heading to the beach to see if the sun is shining in Knokke or it is surfing weather at Bredene.

362 **BELGIUM PIER**

The 5 best
MINI GOLF
COURSES

366 CHALET MINIGOLF

Leopoldpark 1
Ostend
Belgian Coast
+32 (0)59 70 54 37
www.chalet-minigolf.be

Ostend has a beautiful mini golf course hidden in the middle of the Leopoldpark. Thickly planted with trees and bushes, this is a romantic place to play a game. Or you can just sit on the café terrace while your kids have fun.

367 BREDENE

Kapelstraat 10
Bredene
Belgian Coast
+32 (0)59 32 12 77
www.minigolf-bredene.be

Bredene has a charming old mini golf course dating back to 1950. It's a romantic, nostalgic course with crazy paving footpaths and some difficult obstacles to get past.

368 LEOPOLDPARK BLANKENBERGE

Jachthaven
Blankenberge
Belgian Coast
+32 (0)50 41 75 98
www.leopoldpark blankenberge.be

Blankenberge has a classic mini golf course located in a park planted with trees, rockeries and flowers in huge pots. The course has some tricky obstacles along the way and benches where you can rest while waiting for your turn.

369 DUINBERGEN

Duinbergenlaan
Knokke
Belgian Coast
+32 (0)50 51 24 91
www.minigolf
duinbergen.be

Duinbergen has a beautifully-landscaped mini golf course set in a rolling park close to the beach. It has several appealing details like a large windmill and a lighthouse, as well as plenty of benches for when kids begin to flop.

370 MINIGOLF PETIT BOIS

Lejeunelaan
Koksijde
Belgian Coast
+32 (0)58 51 72 11

Here is an authentic mini golf course in a little park shaded by old trees. It is one of the oldest mini golfs on the coast, with landscaped grounds, meandering paths and a little wooden chalet serving drinks.

'T WITHUIS

45 PLACES TO SLEEP

———

The 5 most INSPIRING HOTELS *in Ypres* —— 190

The 5 COOLEST B&BS *in Ypres* —— 192

The 5 best B&BS IN FLANDERS FIELDS —— 194

The 5 most ROMANTIC HOTELS
in Flanders Fields —— 196

The 5 most CHARMING RESIDENCES
in Diksmuide and Veurne —— 198

The 5 most ORIGINAL LODGINGS
in Flanders Fields —— 201

The 5 most ROMANTIC
BEACH LODGINGS —— 204

The 5 most INSPIRING B&BS *at the coast* —— 206

The 5 most HIP PLACES *to stay on the coast* —— 208

The 5 most
INSPIRING HOTELS
in Ypres

371 MAIN STREET HOTEL

Rijselstraat 136
Ypres
Flanders Fields
+32 (0)57 46 96 33
www.mainstreet-
hotel.be

This cool new hotel occupies a red brick building with a small courtyard at the back. It is an odd, fun place crammed with vintage ornaments and old photographs. The six guest rooms are decorated in wildly different styles with whimsical touches like vintage wallpaper and huge bathtubs.

372 ARIANE

Slachthuisstraat 58
Ypres
Flanders Fields
+32 (0)57 21 82 18
www.ariane.be

This family-run hotel occupies an old Flemish-style brick building and a smart modern extension. It has a beautiful modern lobby, a conservatory and an attractive garden with a large terrace overlooking a pond. The bedrooms are spacious and the beds are designed to send you into a deep contented sleep.

373 AMBROSIA

D'Hondtstraat 54
Ypres
Flanders Fields
+32 (0)57 36 63 66
www.ambrosiahotel.be

This is a small hotel in an old brick house with a narrow wooden staircase leading to the bedrooms. It is run by a friendly young couple who will rent you bicycles or even a cool Honda scooter to get out into the countryside. The room rates are very reasonable.

374 ALBION

Sint-Jacobsstraat 28
Ypres
Flanders Fields
+32 (0)57 20 02 20
www.albionhotel.be

Christiane and her daughter Ruth opened this hotel in 2000 in a reconstructed 17th century town house, and added several new rooms in 2014. The lounge is a comfortable place to sit with a local beer while the guest rooms are decorated in a sober modern style.

375 REGINA

Grote Markt 45
Ypres
Flanders Fields
+32 (0)57 21 88 88
www.hotelregina.be

This traditional Flemish hotel is right in the centre of Ypres. It is a charming place to stay with friendly staff and a certain old Belgian charm. The rooms at the front are the most attractive, with views of the mediaeval cloth hall across the street.

371 MAIN STREET HOTEL

The 5
COOLEST B&BS
in Ypres

376 LA PORTE COCHERE

Patersstraat 22
Ypres
Flanders Fields
+32 (0)57 44 69 94
www.laporte
cochere.com

This is an attractive B&B in a reconstructed town house with a huge entrance hall. The rooms are decorated in elegant Flemish style with polished wooden floors and antique furniture. Breakfast is served in a bright conservatory overlooking the back garden. The owners are friendly people who know a lot about the history of Ypres.

377 ALEGRIA

Neerstraat 14
Ypres
Flanders Fields
+32 (0)57 21 41 61
www.alegria-bb.be

Luc Neirynck recently renovated a town house to create a stylish B&B with three spacious rooms designed in contemporary style. He is an exceptionally friendly host who can tell you where to find the best local beers or the most informative tours. He also serves a delicious breakfast which you can eat on a little terrace at the back. The rooms are among the cheapest in town.

378 VILLA VANILLA

Groenestraat 12
Ypres
Flanders Fields
+32 (0)57 21 92 14
www.villavanilla.be

Christa and Christophe run a stylish B&B with four guest rooms in the quiet suburbs. It is a friendly, homely place with a log fire in the bar and a rambling garden where you can sit with a book. You can also borrow bikes to ride out into the countryside.

379 SABBAJON

Boezingepoort-
straat 6
Ypres
Flanders Fields
+32 (0)57 20 30 06
www.sabbajon.be

Joke runs a cool modern B&B in a reconstructed 19th century town house near the centre. The four bedrooms are decorated with bright colours and modern beds. Breakfast is served in the summer in a pretty walled back garden.

380 FIELDS OF GOLD

Rijselstraat 74
Ypres
Flanders Fields
+32 (0)496 81 82 07
www.fieldsofgold.be

Pieter and Natalie run this stylish B&B in a beautifully restored baroque school house. They have a natural food shop on the ground floor that fills the whole house with seductive scents. The four guest rooms are bright and comfortable with creative details such as clawfoot baths and small balconies looking out on the back garden. Nathalie makes a delicious breakfast using fresh produce from local farms.

The 5 best
B&Bs IN
FLANDERS FIELDS

---

381 DE RENTMEESTER-HOEVE

Reningelstplein 5
Reningelst
Flanders Fields
+32 (0)477 37 92 86
www.rentmeester
hoeve.be

This beautiful B&B occupies a reconstructed cottage in the grounds of a destroyed castle. It is run by a friendly young couple who welcome you with a glass of picon, the local aperitif. All four bedrooms are tastefully decorated with wood floors, old chests and oak beams.

382 VARLET FARM

Wallemolenstraat 43
Poelkapelle
Flanders Fields
+32 (0)470 21 16 54
www.varletfarm.com

Dirk Cardoen runs one of the most welcoming B&Bs in the region. He offers coffee and homemade apple cake when you arrive and can tell you everything you need to know about the First World War. His restored farmhouse stands on the site of a German bunker marked on British war maps as Varlet Farm and he has dug up countless relics of the war which he keeps in a private museum in the garage.

383 DE KLAPROOS

Tynecotstraat 26
Passendale
Flanders Fields
+32 (0)51 77 87 53
www.deklaproos.com

Marijke offers self-catering apartments in a house next to Tyne Cot Cemetery with sweeping views of the countryside where the Battle of Passchendaele was fought. She has a large collection of books on the war and can recommend routes for cycling along the Salient. The apartments are quiet once the last tourists have left Tyne Cot, with wooden terraces at the back that overlook the endless rows of headstones.

384 AMADEE

Kortestraat 4
Zandvoorde
Flanders Fields
+32 (0)495 38 21 23
www.amadee.be

Dirk and Inge renovated a ruined farmhouse in the middle of the countryside to create their sublime B&B. They have four stylish bedrooms with bare brick walls, oak beams and cool contemporary furniture. You can sit with a book in front of the fire or relax outside in a hot tub.

385 DE AKKERWINDE

Lange Dreve 12
Zonnebeke
Flanders Fields
+32 (0)478 50 03 57
www.deakkerwinde.be

This is a friendly B&B with simple, comfortable rooms decorated in a romantic style and a big farmhouse table in the dining room where everyone sits together for breakfast. It's not luxurious, but it is an affordable place to stay in the heart of the battlefields, not far from Polygon Wood.

The 5 most
ROMANTIC HOTELS
in Flanders Fields

386 RECOUR

Guido Gezellestraat 7
Poperinge
Flanders Fields
+32 (0)57 33 57 25
www.pegasusrecour.be

This family-owned hotel occupies a 1780 town house that was once a tobacco factory. It has a relaxed, warm feel with a spacious lounge decorated in a comfortable country house style by interior designer Pieter Porters. The eight guest rooms in the old house are furnished with big wooden beds, polished desks and retro baths, while the seven new rooms in the annex have interiors inspired by contemporary designers.

387 MANOIR OGYGIA

Veurnestraat 108
Poperinge
Flanders Fields
+32 (0)57 33 88 38
www.ogygia.be

This little hotel was built in 2003 in the grounds of a 19th century castle on the edge of Poperinge. The nine guest rooms are furnished in a comfortable romantic style with big old cupboards and stylish clawfoot baths. It has a friendly, relaxed atmosphere with chairs dotted around the garden where you can read a book while peacocks strut around.

388 HOTEL REVERIE

Rodebergstraat 26
Westouter
Flanders Fields
+32 (0)57 44 48 19
www.reverie.be

Hotel Reverie is a sublime family hotel in a half-timbered building deep in the Heuvelland countryside. It has spacious bedrooms, a huge garden and hops hanging from the dining room ceiling. The sweeping views across the rolling countryside make this hotel a truly special place.

389 HOTEL HET WETHUYS

Watouplein 2
Watou
Flanders Fields
+32 (0)57 20 60 02
www.wethuys.be

This attractive small hotel occupies a former courthouse overlooking Watou's neat village square. It is run by a friendly couple who have created three comfortable guest rooms. They also run a restaurant where you can eat Flemish specialities. Or you can just sit on the terrace drinking one of the sublime local beers brewed in a building behind the hotel.

390 KASTEELHOF 'T HOOGHE

Meenseweg 481
Ypres
Flanders Fields
+32 (0)57 46 87 87
www.hotelkasteelhof
thooghe.be

This hotel stands on the historic Menin Road in the middle of a wooded area that was once the front line. The building was rebuilt in the 1920s in an English half-timbered style with a romantic rambling garden and a large waterlogged crater at the back. It feels rather old-fashioned, but it has a certain charm, and the location is perfect for getting around the battlefields.

The 5 most
CHARMING RESIDENCES
in Diksmuide and Veurne

391 NOTARISHUYS

Koning
Albertstraat 39
Diksmuide
Flanders Fields
+32 (0)51 50 03 35
www.notarishuys.be

This is a stunning contemporary hotel in a quiet location on the edge of Diksmuide. The young owners Bert and Jessica have created an exceptionally friendly and inspiring place to stay, equipped with smart modern devices and a luxurious sauna. The guest rooms are decorated in a stark minimalist style that adds to the sense of wellbeing.

392 'T WITHUIS

Grote Markt 33
Diksmuide
Flanders Fields
+32 (0)51 50 69 55
www.withuis
diksmuide.be

This is a beautiful B&B located in a reconstructed 18th-century town house on the main square in Diksmuide. The interior has been totally redesigned in a calm modern style with just the occasional antique table or chandelier. This is the perfect location for exploring the battlefield sites of the Yser valley. You can even begin with the concrete bunker in the back garden and the German graffiti on the breakfast room wall.

392 'T WITHUIS

393 THE OLD HOUSE

Zwarte
Nonnenstraat 8
Veurne
Flanders Fields
+32 (0)58 31 19 31
www.theoldhouse.be

Here is a charming B&B in an 18th-century brick house near the lively main square in Veurne. It has the feeling of a family home filled with beautiful furniture, paintings and odd personal touches. The eleven guest rooms vary in size from large rooms looking out on the garden to romantic hideaways beneath the roof beams.

394 AUBERGE DE KLASSE

Astridlaan 3
Veurne
Flanders Fields
+32 (0)479 76 55 12
www.auberge
deklasse.be

This small inn occupies a modest brick town house from 1725 with a romantic English garden. The owner offers you a glass of wine in the garden the moment you step through the door. The three guest rooms are decorated in a warm, comfortable style, while breakfast begins with a glass of freshly-squeezed orange juice.

395 HET SCHALIËNHOF

Zoutenaaiestraat 6
Eggewaartskapelle
Flanders Fields
+32 (0)473 61 54 91
www.schalienhof.be

This restored farmhouse lies out in the countryside surrounded by quiet lanes for cycling. It is a quiet, welcoming place with a rustic kitchen where the owners bake home-made bread every morning and spacious guest rooms decorated in a cool modern style. The beach at Oostduinkerke is a short drive away, but there is nowhere to eat near the farm.

The 5 most
ORIGINAL LODGINGS
in Flanders Fields

396 DE KLOOSTERLOFT

Patersstraat 7
Ypres
Flanders Fields
+32 (0)51 30 42 35
www.dekloosterloft.be

This remarkable two-bedroom loft apartment is located in a brick Carmelite monastery rebuilt in the 1920s. It has retained the old Catholic interior, including the cold tiled floors, vaulted corridors and Neo-Gothic murals. You stay in a spacious apartment with two bedrooms, a sitting room and a kitchen.

397 BROUWERSHUIS

Trappistenweg 23
Watou
Flanders Fields
+32 (0)57 38 88 60
www.brouwershuis.com

The Brouwershuis is a quiet rural B&B hidden behind the high walls of the Sint-Bernardus brewery. The eleven guest rooms occupy the former master brewer's house, where guests can now drink a glass of Sint-Bernardus 12 in the old conservatory. The owner serves an excellent breakfast which includes fresh bread from the local baker. She can tell you about the best cycle routes in the region and perhaps even arrange a tour of the brewery.

398 TALBOT HOUSE

398 TALBOT HOUSE

Gasthuisstraat 43
Poperinge
Flanders Fields
+32 (0)57 33 32 28
www.talbothouse.be

You can spend a night at Talbot House in a room that has barely changed since World War One. The rooms are furnished in a simple style with a bed, a cupboard and a few old books left behind by soldiers. The house is run by a friendly manager who offers guests a cup of tea and a biscuit when they arrive. It may not be luxurious, but it is a deeply moving place to spend a night.

399 'T KOMMIEZENKOT

Abeelseweg 183
Poperinge
Flanders Fields
+32 (0)57 33 23 70
www.kommiezenkot.be

Elvis impersonator Wally and his wife Patty run this quirky hotel in a former customs house on the frontier between Belgium and France. The bedrooms are simple, but comfortable. Each one is named after a customs official who once worked here. You might find the village a bit dull, unless you wander down the road to Wally's Farm, where the owner used to sing Elvis songs deep into the night.

400 GLAMPING ECOCHIQUE

Hellegatstraat 6a
Westouter
Flanders Fields
+32 (0)486 43 02 47
www.ecochique.be

Here is a cool ecological camping experience in the deep countryside where you don't have to give up any home comforts. You stay in a comfortable tent equipped with designer furniture, flat screen TV, wood-burning stove, espresso machine and even a private bathroom. You can borrow modern art to decorate the tent, swim in a heated pool and steam in a sauna.

The 5 most
ROMANTIC
BEACH LODGINGS

---

401 VILLA SELECT

Walckierstraat 7
De Panne
Belgian Coast
+32 (0)58 42 99 00
www.hotelvillaselect.be

This beautiful old Flemish hotel is one of the last on the Belgian coast where you can sleep in a room with a sea view. The guest rooms are spacious and bright with sweeping views of the silver-grey North Sea. The hotel is run by a friendly young couple who lay out a generous breakfast in a bright room overlooking the beach. You can also swim in an indoor pool or sweat in the sauna.

402 MANOIR CARPE DIEM

Prins Karellaan 12
De Haan
Belgian Coast
+32 (0)59 23 32 20
www.manoir
carpediem.com

Claudine and Patrick Deryckere run this gorgeous whitewashed hotel in the quiet beach town of De Haan. The 15 guest rooms are decorated in a warm country house style with little maritime details dotted around. The hotel has a big English garden and a swimming pool that is open in the summer.

403 VILLA LA TOURELLE

Vondellaan 4
De Haan
Belgian Coast
+32 (0)59 23 34 54
www.latourelle.be

This rambling villa with bay windows and a turret is one of the most romantic places to stay on the Belgian coast. The owner Maria Vantorre has decorated the nine bedrooms in a light country style that incorporates parquet floors, baroque beds and white dressers. It's worth asking for room 9 in the turret for the stunning view.

404 MANITOBA

Manitobaplein 11
Blankenberge
Belgian Coast
+32 (0)50 41 12 20
www.hotelmanitoba.
com

This beautiful 1890 mansion dates from the days when Blankenberge was one of the most elegant resorts on the North Sea coast. The building preserves all its old charm, including tiled fireplaces, oak panelling and large mirrors. The friendly owner creates a relaxed atmosphere and serves breakfast in a beautiful back room looking out on the garden.

405 LA PASSION INTERDITE

Graaf de Smet de
Naeyerlaan 16
Ostend
Belgian Coast
+32 (0)473 35 84 01
www.lapassion
interdite.be

This lovely 1910 house is just about the perfect place for a romantic weekend at the beach. It has just two rooms which are furnished in a simple old-fashioned style with big oak wardrobes and chandeliers, along with charming touches like an old wicker basket at the foot of the bed.

The 5 most
INSPIRING B&BS
at the coast

406 EVERGREEN

Koninklijke Baan 197
Koksijde
Belgian Coast
+32 (0)495 12 41 59
www.evergreen
koksijde.be

This gorgeous B&B occupies a modern white house built in Belgian seaside style. The owner Patrick is a charming host who offers three guest rooms in different styles. Each room has a terrace that catches the sun for much of the day. We love the romance of the Sea View room, even if the sea view is just wallpaper.

407 VILLA ELSA

Leopold II Laan 56
Oostduinkerke
Belgian Coast
+32 (0)476 40 91 62
www.villaelsa.be

Villa Elsa is a gorgeous B&B located in a rambling 19th century coastal villa. It is run by a talented interior designer called Els who has created boudoir-style guest rooms furnished with old chairs, plump red velvet cushions and potted plants. Photographers sometimes come here to do fashion shoots. On summer days breakfast is served in a romantic garden.

408 HUYZE ELIMONICA

Euphrosina
Beernaerstraat 39
Ostend
Belgian Coast
+32 (0)479 67 07 09
www.elimonica.be

Filip Deschacht runs a sublime B&B in a gorgeous fin-de-siècle home built in 1899. He spent three years restoring the house and redecorated the rooms with rustic white furniture, contemporary paintings and odd details like jars of seashells. The breakfast is a spectacular spread served at a long wooden table in the basement, or out in the garden if it is warm. There is even a garage across the road where you can park your car.

409 VILLA D'HONDT

Weststraat 92
Blankenberge
Belgian Coast
+32 (0)496 59 39 40
www.villadhondt.com

This is a charming B&B located in a handsome 1904 Art Nouveau house just five minutes from the beach. The downstairs rooms have intriguing frescos painted on linen, along with antique furniture and stained glass windows. The friendly owner provides an excellent breakfast to start the day.

410 PREFECTENHUIS

Leon Spilliaert-
straat 23
Ostend
Belgian Coast
+32 (0)477 26 88 90
www.prefectenhuis.be

Nathalie and Karl opened this stunning B&B opposite Ostend's Leopoldpark in 2014. It occupies an 1890 white mansion with a white stucco hallway and a beautiful wooden staircase. The two guest rooms have a relaxed feel with old wood floors and white furniture, while the bathrooms are fitted with vintage sinks. The room at the front has a balcony looking out on the park, but the room at the back is the one to select if you need quiet.

The 5 most
HIP PLACES
to stay on the coast

---

411 SUITE 17

Ieperstraat 17
Nieuwpoort
Belgian Coast
+32 (0)479 47 47 22
www.suite17.be

Sean Lybeer and Joëlle Swart run a sleek modern B&B that looks like a villain's hideaway in a 1960s James Bond movie. Anyone who admires contemporary design will be thrilled by the vintage chairs, concrete floors and modern Belgian art. It even has a sunny terrace and a narrow swimming pool.

412 BLANCHES VOILES

Albert I laan 320
Zeedijk 113
Nieuwpoort
Belgian Coast
+32 (0)58 62 04 29
www.blanchesvoiles.be

It's hard these days to find a place to stay on the coast with a view of the sea unless you rent a private apartment. But this stylish B&B in an old seafront house has fabulous views from some of the guest rooms. The interiors are furnished with quirky design classics.

413 ITEMS

Konijnendreef 6
Knokke
Belgian Coast
+32 (0)50 60 36 06
www.bea-bb.com

Bea Mombaers runs a sublime B&B in an old farmhouse with a thatched roof, wild garden and swimming pool. She has furnished the three guest rooms with an eclectic collection of 1950s vintage chairs and lamps from her interior design shop.

414 **BONNE AUBERGE**

Maria
Hendrikalaan 10
De Haan
Belgian Coast
+32 (0)59 23 31 61
www.hotelbonne
auberge.be

This is a gorgeous beach hotel located in a romantic half-timbered villa. The interior is decorated in a bold modern style, while the lounge is a relaxed spot to flop down with a good book. We love the friendly owners, the odd details dotted around the place and the fabulous breakfast.

415 **VILLA ALTA**

Elisabethstraat 34
Blankenberge
Belgian Coast
+32 (0)498 16 06 06
www.villa-alta.be

This is a spacious apartment for two in a grand Blankenberge building dating from the late 19th century. You can live comfortably here for a few days in your own private home with wood floors, marble fireplaces and views of the sea. It also has a kitchen, a little balcony and a private sauna.

411 **SUITE 17**

BAYERENWALD

25 ACTIVITIES
IN FLANDERS FIELDS

——————

The 5 best **BREWERIES** *to visit* ———————— 212

The 5 best **NATURE RESERVES** ———————— 214

The 5 best **CYCLE TRIPS** *in Flanders Fields* ——— 216

The 5 most enjoyable
EVENTS IN THE WESTHOEK ———————— 218

The 5 most impressive
RELICS OF OTHER WARS ———————— 220

The 5 best
BREWERIES
to visit

---

416 BROUWERIJ KAZEMATTEN
Bollingstraat 1
Ypres
Flanders Fields
+32 (0)57 46 94 62
*www.brasserie
kazematten.be*

This new brewery is still something of a secret. It occupies ancient 17th century casemates below the Ypres town walls where British troops printed a humorous trench newspaper called *The Wipers Times.* The brewhouse was launched here in 2014 by the people who own Sint-Bernardus in Watou.

417 DE DOLLE BROUWERS
Roeselarestraat 12
Esen
Flanders Fields
+32 (0)51 50 27 81
www.dedollebrouwers.be

Here is a fantastic local brewery launched in 1980 by three friends who called themselves *De Dolle Brouwers*, or The Mad Brewers. They took over a dilapidated 19th century brewery in the village of Esen near Diksmuide and launched a limited range of six bottled beers.

418 DE PLUKKER
Elverdingseweg 16
Poperinge
Flanders Fields
www.plukker.be

Here is an innovative brewery set up in Poperinge in 2010. It is run by two enthusiasts who make their beers using organic hops grown on a local farm. They have already created some exceptional beers including the lovely Keikoppen. The brewery has a small tasting room open on Saturday afternoons.

419 DE STRUISE BROUWERS

Het Oud Schooltje
Kasteelstraat 50
Oostvleteren
Flanders Fields
struise.com

Some of the most distinctive beers in Belgium come from a small craft brewery in Oostvleteren begun by four friends in 2001. They brew a range of about 30 beers with distinctive tastes and curious names like Pannenpot and Tsjeeses. Some of the brewing is done in an old village schoolhouse in Oostvleteren, where you can also taste the beers.

420 SINT-BERNARDUS

Trappistenweg 23
Watou
Flanders Fields
+32 (0)57 38 80 21
www.sintbernardus.be

The Sint-Bernardus brewery began brewing in the little border town of Watou in 1946. They used to brew Trappist beer for the monks at Westvleteren. Now they brew Sint-Bernardus beers which are close in taste to Westvleteren, but much easier to find. The brewery organises tours and sells crates of beer in the shop.

416 BROUWERIJ KAZEMATTEN

The 5 best
NATURE RESERVES

---

421 DE BLANKAART
Iepersteenweg 56
Woumen
Flanders Fields
+32 (0)51 54 52 44

You need a good pair of boots to hike through the Blankaart nature reserve north of Ypres. This is a beautiful area of marshes, meadows and ponds that is often flooded in the winter. You can follow a 10-kilometre walking trail through the reserve where you often see rare migrating birds.

422 DE PALINGBEEK
Palingbeekstraat 18
Ypres
Flanders Fields
+32 (0)57 20 56 72
www.depalingbeek.be

The Palingbeek estate lies just a few miles out of Ypres on high ground to the south. This was an area of fierce fighting along the banks of a disused canal during the First World War. It has taken many years to restore the landscape and replant the trees. Now it is a beautiful area of woods where rabbits run wild.

423 POLYGOONBOS

Lange Dreef
Zonnebeke
Flanders Fields

This area of woodland east of Ypres was reduced to a few dead trees at the end of the war. It has been carefully replanted with oak and beech so that now it is hard to imagine that it was ever a battlefield. Yet deep in the wood you come across several bunkers along with a large military cemetery where more than 2,000 soldiers are buried.

424 PLOEGSTEERT WOOD

Rue de la Munque
Ploegsteert
Flanders Fields

It sounds like a Flemish name, but Ploegsteert lies across the language border in French-speaking Belgium. This is a silent, forgotten spot where you can follow rough trails that were given the names of London streets during the war. You occasionally come across overgrown concrete bunkers and unexpected cemeteries deep in these mysterious woods.

425 VRIJBOS

E. de Grootelaan
Houthulst
Flanders Fields

An old area of woodlands called Houthulstbos was totally destroyed at the end of the First World War. The land was taken over by the Belgian army as a base for disposing of old shells. One hundred years on, the army is still dealing with the "iron harvest" of deadly shells dug up every year, leaving just a small area called Vrijbos where people can walk and cycle. Some rare birds have made a habitat in this scarred woodland.

The 5 best
CYCLE TRIPS
in Flanders Fields

---

426 YPRES TO ESSEX FARM

It only takes about 15 minutes to ride from Ypres out to Essex Farm where John McCrae wrote the poem In Flanders Fields. Another 15 minutes brings you to the Calvaire Breton monument, near the spot where the first gas attack happened. Then you can follow quiet roads back into Ypres passing close to at least six war cemeteries. Follow numbers: 30, 33, 34, 35, 24, 64, 26 and 34.

427 YPRES TO HILL 62

A slightly tougher cycle ride takes you out to the ridge south of Ypres, where you find monuments, museums, cemeteries and craters. The best route to take follows an abandoned canal out of Ypres before climbing the gentle slope up to De Palingbeek, where you can stop at a café before continuing to Hill 62. You should allow half a day for this trip. Follow numbers: 30, 36, 38, 47, 46, 44, 42, 55, 56, 32 and 33.

428 YPRES TO ZONNEBEKE

You can cycle from Ypres along quiet country roads that lead uphill to the little town of Zonnebeke. The route takes you across the gently sloping fields where millions of soldiers fought in the summer of 1917. Once you have reached Zonnebeke, you can return to Ypres by a longer route that runs near to Polygon Wood. A short detour here brings you to a café. Follow numbers: 33, 32, 56, 31, 41, 42, 55, 40 and 38.

429 ZONNEBEKE TO PASSENDALE

This is one of the most interesting cycle routes in the Ypres area. It follows an old railway line that was used in 1917 by Australian troops trying to capture Passchendaele. Starting at the old station in Zonnebeke, you can follow the line past several explanation boards as well as the remains of a concrete bunker. After two kilometres, leave the railway line to look at Tyne Cot Cemetery and then follow the quiet roads that lead up to Passendale. Follow numbers: 31, 30, 36, 29 and 35.

430 WIJTSCHATE TO MESEN

The village of Wijtschate stands on the ridge where 19 mines were detonated in the summer of 1917. You can follow a circular route from the village across fields dotted with craters and small cemeteries. The route takes you close to the Pool of Peace crater and the beautiful Irish Peace Park. Follow numbers: 50, 9, 52 and 50.

The 5 most enjoyable
EVENTS IN THE WESTHOEK

---

431 DE GEVLEUGELDE STAD
Esplanade
Ypres
Flanders Fields
www.acci.be

The cobbled streets of Ypres are filled with clowns, mime artists and acrobats during the annual festival of street art. More than 70 international companies put on free shows in several outdoor locations such as the ramparts and the main square. The organisers make sure that there are also indoor venues in case it rains over the weekend.

432 WATOU ART FESTIVAL
Watou
Flanders Fields
www.kunstenfestival
watou.be

The pretty little border village of Watou holds an inspiring art festival every summer featuring poets and contemporary artists. You can follow an art trail through the village to discover exciting and sometimes disturbing art installations in unexpected locations, from an abandoned monastery to an overgrown farmyard.

433 DRANOUTER FOLK FESTIVAL
Dranouter
Flanders Fields
+32 (0)57 44 69 33
www.festival
dranouter.be

The little border village of Dranouter has been holding a folk festival in early August since 1975. It started as a modest affair in a school playground, but grew into one of the biggest folk festivals in Europe, attracting famous bands from Britain and Ireland as well as home-grown Flemish folk. While some festivals are struggling to survive, Dranouter continues to draw fans to a remote field in Flanders for three days of gentle music.

434 POPERINGE BEER FESTIVAL
Poperinge
Flanders Fields
www.poperinge
bierfestival.be

About twenty small brewers show off their latest craft beers at the annual Poperinge Beer Festival. Organised by the Poperinge Beer Tasting Society, it is held in the old-fashioned Hotel Belfort on the main square. This is a friendly event that attracts beer enthusiasts from all over Europe.

435 YPRES CATS' PARADE
Ypres
Flanders Fields
www.kattenstoet.be

This is an odd parade featuring a procession of giant cats held every three years. Launched in 1955 by the local mayor, it was intended to create a sense of local pride in a town that was still struggling to recover from the war. The parade has its origins in a cruel mediaeval festival in which cats were tossed from the belfry.

The 5 most impressive
RELICS OF OTHER WARS

---

436 COMMANDOBUNKER KEMMEL
Lettingstraat
Kemmel
(Heuvelland)
Flanders Fields
+32 (0)57 45 04 55

Not many people know about the secret Nato bunker built below the Kemmelberg hill during the Cold War. Once a well-kept military secret, the vast underground complex is now open to the public on Tuesdays and Saturdays. It's a strange place that feels like a James Bond movie set. You see huge military maps on the wall, endless metal cabinets and rows of old telephones from the 1950s, while above ground there is nothing apart from a fake house hidden in the woods.

437 FORT NAPOLEON
Vuurtorenweg
Ostend
Belgian Coast
+32 (0)59 32 00 48
www.fortnapoleon.be

Take the free ferry across Ostend harbour and follow the signs to Fort Napoleon. You come to a massive brick fortress built in the dunes by Napoleon and occupied by German soldiers in the Second World War. The building was brilliantly restored in 2006 by the Ostend architects Govaert & Vanhoutte as a fortress museum and upmarket restaurant.

438 RAVERSIJDE

Nieuwpoortse-
steenweg 636
Ostend
Belgian Coast
www.west-vlaanderen.
be/raversijde

This is a sprawling outdoor museum that includes a large section of Hitler's Atlantic Wall. Huge anti-aircraft guns can be seen from the coast tram while trenches and underground tunnels are concealed in the dunes. This astonishing complex includes furnished German bunkers and an accordion left behind by Rommel when he inspected the site in 1943.

439 THE SIEGE OF YPRES

Vandenpeereboom-
plein
Ypres
Flanders Fields

A huge painting of the Siege of Ypres in 1383 was recently restored and hung in St Martin's Cathedral. Painted in 1667 by Joris Liebaert, it shows Ypres being attacked by an army made up of troops from England and Ghent. The city was eventually saved after people prayed to the Madonna of Thuyne.

440 FLUGPLATZ PESELHOEK

Westvleterseweg
Poperinge
Flanders Fields

A mysterious brick tower stands in a field near the road from Poperinge to Westvleteren. It is all that remains of an airfield built by the Germans in 1940 but abandoned a few months later. Some people believe it was a fake airfield built to deceive the Allies.

DE HAAN

THE 25 PROMINENT PEOPLE IN FLANDERS FIELDS AND THE BELGIAN COAST

———————

The 5 most FAMOUS PEOPLE
who died in Flanders Fields ———————————— 224

The 5 most SIGNIFICANT WOMEN ———————— 226

The 5 people who have SHAPED
FLANDERS FIELDS ———————————————— 228

The 5 most famous YPRES SURVIVORS ———— 230

The 5 people who FELL IN LOVE
with the Belgian coast ———————————————— 232

The 5 most
FAMOUS PEOPLE
who died in Flanders Fields

441 JOHN MCCRAE
Essex Farm Cemetery
Diksmuidseweg
Boezinge
Flanders Fields

John McCrae was a Canadian doctor who worked in a field hospital near the Ypres canal. He treated Canadians wounded during the German gas attacks on 22 April 1915. A few days later, he wrote the poem *In Flanders Fields* that came to symbolise the senseless slaughter. The poem led to the poppy being adopted as a symbol of remembrance across the world.

442 HEDD WYN
Artillery Wood
Cemetery
Boezinge
Flanders Fields
Plot II, Row F,
Grave 11

The Welsh poet Hedd Wyn was killed in heavy rain on 31 July 1917 during the Battle of Passchendaele. Once a sheep farmer, he mostly wrote romantic nature poetry, but also composed several war poems including *Rhyfel* (War) which begins with the line: 'Why must I live in this grim age?' Six weeks after his death, he was awarded the bard's chair at the National Eisteddfod.

443 FRANCIS LEDWIDGE

Artillery Wood
Cemetery
Boezinge
Flanders Fields
Plot II, Row B,
Grave 5

The Irish nature poet Francis Ledwidge was killed on the same day as Hedd Wyn. He was working with an Irish battalion laying a road in preparation for the assault on Passchendaele. Ledwidge was blown to bits along with five other soldiers while drinking a mug of tea in a shell hole. He is buried in the same cemetery as Hedd Wyn.

444 GEORGE LLEWELYN DAVIES

Voormezele
Enclosure No. 3
Ruusschaartstraat
Voormezele
Flanders Fields

Buried outside the village of Voormezele, south of Ypres, George Llewelyn Davies was one of five brothers who inspired J. M. Barrie's children's story *Peter Pan*. He was 10 years old when Barrie wrote the story, and possibly served as the model for 'the boy who never grew up'. George was 21 when he died of a head wound on 15 March 1915.

445 JAMES DUFFY

Vlamertinge
Cemetery
Flanders Fields
Plot I, Row F,
Grave 14

James Duffy was a tough Irish runner who represented Canada at the 1912 Stockholm Olympics and won the 1914 Boston Marathon. He celebrated the victory by lighting a cigarette and drinking a bottle of beer. He was due to represent Canada at the 1916 Berlin Olympics but then war broke out. Duffy was wounded on 23 April 1915 in an attack near Langemark and died the next day.

The 5 most
SIGNIFICANT WOMEN

---

446 MARIE TACK

Villa Marietta
IJzerdijk 18
Nieuwkapelle
Flanders Fields

Madame Tack was living in a large country house called Villa Marietta on the west bank of the Yser canal as the German army advanced. She refused to leave her home, even though it lay in the front line between the Belgian and German trenches, and took food and cigarettes to the Belgian soldiers in the trenches. Known as 'the Soldiers' Mother' or the 'Lady of the Trenches', she received a Belgian knighthood in 1916.

447 EDITH WHARTON

'We had seen other ruined towns, but none like this,' wrote Edith Wharton when she visited the ruins of Ypres on 21 June 1915. She had set off on a tour of the Western Front to report on the war for a New York newspaper. Passing through Poperinge, she found an empty classroom in an abandoned convent with neat rows of lace cushions on the desks. Wharton hoped her reports would persuade America to enter the war, but her homeland remained neutral until April 1917.

448 GINGER

Grote Markt 16
Poperinge
Flanders Fields

Eliane Cossey was the youngest daughter of a shoemaker in Poperinge. Born in 1902, she was 12 when soldiers began to arrive in the town. Her enterprising father turned his shop into a café called A la Poupée and installed a piano. The soldiers came here to drink but also to flirt with the striking red-haired girl they called Ginger. She moved to London after the war and died in a German air raid in 1942.

449 NELLIE SPINDLER

Lijssenthoek
Cemetery
Boescheepseweg 35A
Poperinge
Flanders Fields
Plot XVI, Row A,
Grave 3
www.lijssenthoek.be

Nurse Nellie Spindler is the only woman among the 10,783 men buried in Lijssenthoek Cemetery. She was killed by an exploding shell while treating wounded soldiers on the first day of the Battle of Passchendaele on 21 August 1917.

450 GERTRUDE JECKELL

The war cemeteries of Belgium and France were designed to remind visitors of quiet English country gardens. The landscape gardener Gertrude Jeckell was called on to advise on the best cottage garden plants and red roses to plant. The Commonwealth War Graves Commission still employs about one hundred gardeners in the Ypres area including four employed full-time at Tyne Cot Cemetery.

The 5 people who have
SHAPED
FLANDERS FIELDS

451 RENÉ COLAERT

René Colaert served as burgomaster of Ypres from 1900 to 1921. He witnessed the destruction of his town during the war and played an important role in its postwar reconstruction. While many British politicians, including Winston Churchill, wanted to preserve the ruined town as a war memorial, Colaert supported the local citizens who just wanted to rebuild their homes.

452 JULES COOMANS

Appointed city architect of Ypres in 1895, Coomans was responsible for the restoration of several historic buildings before the outbreak of war, including the cloth hall and belfry. He saw his work destroyed during the war, but returned to Ypres once peace was restored to work on rebuilding the town. He constructed dozens of buildings in Ypres gothic style, sometimes adding little touches of his own.

453 **ANTONY D'YPRES**

Maurice Antony was a Belgian photographer who signed his works 'Antony d'Ypres'. He was living in Ypres when war broke out and took famous photographs of the cloth hall in ruins which were published in British newspapers. He returned to Ypres after the war to photograph the ruined cloth hall and the earliest battlefield tourists, before moving with his family to Ostend.

454 **FABIAN WARE**

Elverdingsestraat 82
Ypres
Flanders Fields
www.cwgc.org

While the war was still being fought, Fabian Ware came up with his plan to build war cemeteries. His proposals led to the creation of the Commonwealth War Graves Commission which now maintains cemeteries all over the world, including 150 in the Ypres area. The Commission has its North European headquarters in Ypres, not far from Ypres Reservoir Cemetery.

455 **PIET CHIELENS**

Piet Chielens grew up in the West Flanders village of Reningelst surrounded by war cemeteries and shell craters. He became an expert on the history and poetry of the Ypres Salient and was appointed conservator of the In Flanders Field Museum. He gave the new museum its unique identity and supervised the reorganisation in 2013 when the main focus shifted to the landscape around Ypres.

The 5 most famous
YPRES SURVIVORS

---

456 **ADOLF HITLER**
Mesen
Flanders Fields

Adolf Hitler served in the trenches of Flanders in a Bavarian regiment. He was stationed near the town of Mesen and in quiet moments made drawings and watercolour paintings of local buildings. He returned to the Ypres area for a two day tour in June 1940 when he visited the Menin Gate and the German cemetery at Langemark.

457 **WINSTON CHURCHILL**
Place de la Rabecque
Ploegsteert
Flanders Fields

Winston Churchill volunteered to serve in the trenches in 1915 after the failure of his bold plan to capture the Dardanelles. He was stationed at Ploegsteert Wood in 1916. A curious plaque on Ploegsteert town hall shows a cigar-smoking Churchill standing dangerously exposed above a British trench.

458 SIEGFRIED SASSOON

Menin Gate
Ypres
Flanders Fields

The war poet Siegfried Sassoon fought in the Battle of Passchendaele in 1917 and wrote about his experiences in the poem *Mud and Rain*. He survived the war and returned to Ypres in 1927, soon after the Menin Gate was built, and later wrote the bitter anti-war poem *On passing the new Menin Gate*.

459 EDMUND BLUNDEN

The poet Edmund Blunden took part in the Battle of Passchendaele in the summer of 1917. He wrote about the battle in the poem *Third Ypres* in which he described his reaction on noticing field mice in the thick of battle. Other poems refer to places around Ypres like Vlamertinghe Castle. Blunden published the war memoir *Undertones of War* in 1928 and remained haunted by his experiences for the rest of his life.

460 ERICH MARIA REMARQUE

The German writer Erich Maria Remarque was sent to the German trenches on 13 July 1917 just as the British prepared to launch the Battle of Passchendaele. He spent some time in the rear lines digging trenches and was hit by shrapnel on 31 July. Remarque recovered in a hospital in Osnabrück, but never returned to the trenches.

5 people who
FELL IN LOVE
with the Belgian coast

---

461 LEOPOLD II

Albert I-promenade
Ostend
Belgian Coast

King Leopold II's personal colony in the Congo yielded enormous profits which he spent largely on architecture and urban projects. The town of Ostend received generous funding to build a grand railway station and an impressive promenade. The king also built a royal villa in the dunes and helped to finance the construction of a tramline along the entire coastline. A statue of Leopold on the promenade is occasionally drenched in red paint in protest at his exploitation of the Congo.

462 LÉON SPILLIAERT

Romestraat 11
Ostend
Belgian Coast
+32 (0)59 50 81 18
www.muzee.be

Léon Spilliaert is a strangely neglected artist who spent most of his life in Ostend. Unable to sleep at night, Spilliaert went on lonely night walks along the promenade, then returned to his studio to paint melancholy scenes of empty restaurants out of season and haunted figures in dark Art Nouveau interiors. Some of his best paintings now hang in the Mu.ZEE.

463 ALBERT EINSTEIN

Shakespearelaan 5
De Haan
Belgian Coast

Albert Einstein and his family moved to De Haan in 1933 to escape the Nazi terror. The famous scientist rented the left wing of a small villa called Savoyarde in the Shakespearelaan. During his six-month stay, Einstein met James Ensor and was photographed by the Ypres photographer Maurice Antony. You can find a statue of Einstein seated on a bench in the small park at the end of Normandielaan.

464 MARVIN GAYE

Albert I-
promenade 77
Ostend
Belgian Coast
www.marvingaye.be

The American singer Marvin Gaye took the ferry from Southampton to Ostend in 1981 to cure his alcohol and sex addiction. He went for long walks along the windswept Albert I-promenade and played darts in a local fisherman's bar. He described Ostend as 'a beat back in tempo' and wrote the hit song *Sexual Healing* during his stay. A bronze statue stands on the Albert I-promenade in front of the dull Residence Jane where he composed his song.

465 ARNO

www.arno.be

The Belgian rock singer Arno Hintjens was born in Ostend in 1949, but moved to Brussels when he was young. He sings boozy, sexy songs in a mixture of English, French and Ostend dialect. Listen to his 1965 single *Les Filles du bord de mer* to get an idea of his raw talent.

DE LUSTIGE VELODROOM

35 RANDOM NOTES AND UNUSUAL FACTS

The 5 best MAPS AND GUIDES —— —— 236

The 5 most exciting THINGS FOR KIDS
in the Westhoek ————————— 238

The 5 WILDEST THINGS TO DO
at the coast——————————— 240

The 5 greatest EVENTS IN THE HISTORY
of the coast——————————— 242

The 5 STRANGEST SIGHTS
at the coast——————— — —— 244

The 5 best WEBSITES on Flanders Fields ——— 246

The 5 most INSPIRING EVENTS
from 2014 to 2018 ——————— 248

The 5 best

MAPS AND GUIDES

466 MAJOR AND MRS HOLT'S BATTLEFIELD GUIDE TO YPRES SALIENT AND PASSCHENDAELE

This book is an essential guide to all the important World War One sites in Flanders Fields. First published in 1995, it describes several day trips by car around the Ypres area. This is the ideal guide for those interested in battlefields, monuments and cemeteries, with a useful folding map at the back.

467 FIETSNETWERK WESTHOEK ZUID

Most people visit Flanders Fields by car or coach, but you get a more intimate experience if you walk or cycle through the landscape. It used to be difficult to find quiet routes to follow, but Westhoek tourist office has published new maps that make it easy to get around. The best map for the Ypres area is the Fietsnetwerk Westhoek Zuid, which helps you plan a route using the network of bike nodes developed in Flanders. The map indicates war cemeteries, woodlands, museums, bike-friendly cafes and even farm shops.

468 WANDELNETWERK IEPERBOOG

This is an excellent map for planning short walks in the Ypres area. It can be used to plan walks around places like Ypres, Hill 60 and Hooge Crater, though it doesn't extend as far as the Messines Ridge or Passchendaele. The walks are marked by the same system of nodes as bike routes.

469 YPRES AND THE BATTLES OF YPRES

www.archive.org

The war was only just over when the Michelin tyre company published a series of guides to the Western Front, including one to Ypres published in 1919. It contains fascinating descriptions of the battlefields written at a time when the towns were still rubble and cemeteries were nothing more than fields of wooden crosses. Now available as a free digital download.

470 WALKING THE SALIENT

The Ypres battlefields make more sense when you hike across the fields in the footsteps of the soldiers. This book written by Paul Reed and first published in 1998 describes 12 walks in the battlefields located along the range of low hills that run from Kemmel to Passendale.

The 5 most exciting
THINGS FOR KIDS
in the Westhoek

---

471 BELLEWAERDE

Meenseweg 497
Ypres
Flanders Fields
+32 (0)57 46 86 86
www.bellewaerde.be

Bellewaerde theme park stands on the site of the First World War battlefields. It started out in 1954 as a bird park, but slowly evolved into a sprawling theme park with roller coasters and wild water rides. It seems strange to come across such a place in the middle of an old war zone. But kids love it all the same.

472 PASSCHENDAELE MEMORIAL MUSEUM

Berten Pilstraat 5A
Zonnebeke
Flanders Fields
+32 (0)51 77 04 41
www.passchendaele.be

Children absolutely love the new war museum at Zonnebeke, which is considered much more exciting than In Flanders Fields. They can put on helmets, wear uniforms and even take a sniff of poison gas. They also enjoy exploring the underground dugouts and running through the reconstructed trenches.

473 ICE MOUNTAIN

Capellestraat 16
Komen
Flanders Fields
+32 (0)56 55 45 40
www.ice-mountain.com

You can take your kids skiing near Ypres on impressive artificial ski runs covered with thick layers of cold snow. The long run is for experienced skiers, but a short run is designed for kids who are just beginning.

474 TORTELBOS

Pannenhuisstraat
Ypres
Flanders Fields

This small wooded estate just outside Ypres stands on the site of two 19th century castles destroyed in the First World War. The woodland has only recently been replanted and is now occupied by an adventure park where kids can play on a wooden ship and scramble up rope ladders.

475 VERS VAN DE HOEVE

Wulvergemstraat 23
Wijtschate
Flanders Fields
+32 (0)57 44 47 54

You can stop to pick up a little pot of home-made ice cream at several farms around Ypres. This one lies on the road to Lone Tree Cemetery and the Pool of Peace. The farmer's wife is in the shop selling her delicious ice cream on Wednesday, Friday and Saturday.

The 5
WILDEST THINGS
TO DO *at the coast*

---

476 SAND YACHTING

Dynastielaan 20
De Panne
Belgian Coast
+32 (0)58 42 08 08
www.rsyc.be

When the wind is right, you can take a ride on a sand yacht along a 30-kilometre stretch of beach from De Panne to Dunkirk. The sport was brought to De Panne in 1898 by the Dumont brothers using sleek land yachts that could reach speeds of over 100 kilometres an hour.

477 SURFING

Zeedijk 50
Zeebrugge
Belgian Coast
+32(0)50 54 76 59
www.icarussurfclub.be

You can find several surf clubs along the windswept Belgian coast where hardy surfers squeeze into wetsuits to ride the North Sea waves. The Icarus surf school is a cool club based in a wooden cabin on Zeebrugge beach.

478 DE LUSTIGE VELODROOM

Blankenberge Beach
Blankenberge
Belgian Coast
www.delustige velodroom.be

This old wooden velodrome has been standing on the beach near Blankenberge pier since 1933. It is one of the strangest seaside attractions in the world. The bicycles are eccentric constructions that are almost impossible to ride along the bumpy wooden cycle track. Kids love to try out the bikes, or just stand at the side watching the fun.

479 **WAVEFUN**

+32 (0)483 22 40 42
www.wavefun.be

Bart Lux is the person to contact if you are looking for something wild to do at the sea. He runs a small company called WaveFun in Blankenberge harbour where he organises jetski excursions out to sea. He also take groups on tours of the Uitkerkse polders on sturdy Finnish kick bikes.

480 **SEAFRONT**

Vismijnstraat 7
Zeebrugge
Belgian Coast
+32 (0)50 55 14 15
www.seafront.be

The huge industrial sheds in Zeebrugge where fish used to be auctioned have been turned into a maritime theme park. The main attractions are two vessels moored out in the harbour, including a former Soviet submarine from the Cold War era.

477 PADDLING IN ZEEBRUGGE

478 DE LUSTIGE VELODROOM

The 5 greatest
EVENTS IN THE HISTORY
of the coast

---

481 OSTEND SIEGE

The Spanish army besieged Ostend for four years during the Revolt of the Netherlands leaving more than 80,000 people killed. The siege finally ended in 1604 when the exhausted Dutch army surrendered the town.

482 THE RAILWAY ARRIVES

The railway line from Brussels to Ostend was completed by 1838 and the Belgian royal family soon began to spend their summers at the coast. A new railway station was built in 1913 in a grand classical style inspired by the palaces of Louis XIV.

483 THE STEAMSHIPS ARRIVE

The first ferry sailed from Ostend to Dover in 1846 opening up an important link between Britain and Continental Europe. The last ferry left Ostend harbour for England on 25 April 1997 and the port now looks rather lifeless.

484 VINDICTIVE RAID

One of the most daring raids of the First World War happened in 1918 when the British warship Vindictive attacked the German submarine base at Zeebrugge. The Vindictive was eventually sunk in Ostend harbour, where the wreck remained until 1920. The bows of the ship are now preserved as a strange monument in Ostend harbour.

485 BEAUFORT 01

The art curator Willy Van den Bussche brought exciting new art to the Belgian coast when he launched Beaufort 01 in 2003. Suddenly contemporary art started to appear in unexpected locations along the beach or in the dunes. The final Beaufort festival was held in 2012, but the coastline remains dotted with sculptures from the four events.

The 5
STRANGEST SIGHTS
at the coast

---

486 BLANKENBERGE BEACH HUTS

Blankenberge beach
Blankenberge
Belgian Coast

You can still see several jaunty bathing machines in the streets of Blankenberge and on the beach. These stripey wooden cabins with four metal wheels were a British invention to take swimmers into the sea. The first ones appeared on Blankenberge beach in 1838, but the ones you see now are replicas made in about 1940.

487 PEERDEVISSCHER

Oostduinkerke
Belgian Coast
visitor.koksijde.be

You sometimes see shrimp fishermen riding huge workhorses through the streets of Oostduinkerke. It is one of the strangest sights on the coast. Dressed in bright yellow oilskins, they ride through the sea dragging vast nets designed to catch small grey shrimps. The fishermen are now listed by UNESCO as part of the world's intangible cultural heritage.

488 SOEPBOER

They are not too common any more, but you still see old vans driving around the Belgian resorts in the early morning selling homemade soup to summer residents. They announce their arrival with a little bell that brings people out onto the street with big saucepans.

489 LIFEGUARDS

Belgian lifeguards sit on platforms high above the beach dressed in red waterproof trousers and anoraks. They are on the lookout for anyone who swims out beyond the markers. As soon as someone strays into danger, the lifeguards blow several times on a brass hunting horn. It is one of the defining sounds of a summer at the Belgian coast.

490 NEW YEAR SWIM

www.nieuwjaarsduik.be

More than 5,000 people gather on Ostend beach every year in early January to rush into the icy North Sea for a quick dip. It has become a fun local tradition that brings out the eccentric charm of the Ostend people. You can sign up online to take part if you are brave enough.

The 5 best
WEBSITES
on Flanders Fields

---

491 FLANDERS FIELDS
www.flandersfields.be

This is an outstanding site in four languages created by the province of West Flanders for the 100th anniversary of the First World War. It has a vast amount of information on war sites in the region, along with exhibitions, events and places to stay.

492 COMMONWEALTH WAR GRAVES COMMISSION
www.cwgc.org

The Commonwealth War Graves Commission has created a database with information on every soldier killed in the two world wars. You can also find out about the cemetery where a soldier is buried and sometimes even download a copy of the death certificate.

493 THE GREAT WAR
www.greatwar.co.uk

Joanna Legg has created a rich and fascinating website on the First World War which includes extensive information on the Ypres Salient. Her website is particularly good for people who want a clear account of the military background and the war relics in the area.

494 GREAT WAR IN FLANDERS FIELDS

www.wo1.be

This website created by the West Flanders government has a vast amount of information on the war in Flanders. It is packed with intriguing details, including lists of bunkers, sites that are being excavated and memorial plaques in remote villages. Most of the information is available in English, although some of the longer articles are only in Dutch.

495 WORLD WAR ONE BATTLEFIELDS

www.ww1battlefields. co.uk

Alan Jennings has created a fascinating website on the First World War battlefields including the Ypres Salient. It includes clear maps that you can use to navigate around the war sites as well as historic photographs and odd mementoes like a 1928 ticket advertising tours of the Flanders battlefields.

The 5 most
INSPIRING EVENTS
from 2014 to 2018

---

496 THE NAME LIST
4 AUGUST 2014
Grote Markt 34
Ypres
Flanders Fields
+32 (0)57 23 92 20
www.inflandersfields.be

Many cultural events are being organised in Belgium to mark the anniversary of the First World War. At In Flanders Fields Museum, the names of soldiers who died in the region will be projected on the museum wall on the 100th anniversary of the day when they died. The first names will appear on 4 August, while the final names will be seen on 11 November 2018.

497 LIGHT FRONT 1914
17 OCTOBER 2014
Kustweg 1
Nieuwpoort
Belgian Coast
www.gonewest.be

This is an ambitious project to create a line of torches running along the Western Front from the beach at Nieuwpoort to the French border at Ploegsteert. Some 8,750 volunteers are needed to form the line, including 1,280 to mark out the 13 km front line around Ypres. The Ostend rock singer Arno is due to give a concert at the end of the day at the sluice complex in Nieuwpoort.

498 SHELL SHOCK

Munt
Brussels
+32 (0)2 229 12 00
www.lamonnaie.be

The Brussels opera house is to stage a new opera titled Shell Shock by the Belgian composer Nicholas Lens with words by Nick Cave and choreography by Sidi Larbi Cherkaoui. The composer aims to portray the suffering of ordinary people caught up in the war.

499 CHRISTMAS TRUCE FOOTBALL MATCH

26 DECEMBER 2014
Ypres
Flanders Fields

A football match between Britain and Germany is due to be played on the 100th anniversary of the 1914 Christmas Truce. It will be held on a new Premier League pitch in Ypres. The original football game is believed to have been held in a frozen field near Ploegsteert.

500 LAST POST ANNIVERSARY

9 JULY 2015
Menin Gate
Ypres
Flanders Fields

A major ceremony will be held at the Menin Gate in 2015 to mark the 30,000th anniversary of the playing of the Last Post. The mournful bugle call was first sounded below the gate soon after it was completed in 1928.

BREDENE BEACH

INDEX

't Binnenhuys	56	Auberge De Klasse	200	Bredene Minigolf	186
't Groote Huys	63	Auberge		Bridge House	
't Kleine Rijsel	53	de la Brique d'Or	23	Cemetery	109
't Kommiezenkot	203	Auberge du Vert Mont	23	Brooding Soldier	139
't Patéwinkeltje/De Veurn'		Baai van Heist	164	Brouwerij	
Ambachtse	47	Babies	176	Kazematten	212
't Sparhof	22	Bandaghem Cemetery	113	Brouwershuis	201
't Waterhuis	39	Bayernwald	117	Café Botteltje	64
't Werftje	37	Bea Items	81	Café de la Paix	21
't Withuis	198	Beauvoorde	148	Café de Paris	27
't Zoet Genot	42	Belfry Ypres	144	Café Manuscript	64
1392 posts	111	Belgium Pier		Calimero	79
1955 Mine Crater	127	Brasserie	62, 184	Callebert	74
Albert and Elisabeth-		Belle Epoque Centrum	162	Capella	17
statues	98	Bellewaerde	238	Casino	47
Albert I monument	177	Bethlehem Farm East		Caterpillar Crater	121
Albion	191	Cemetery	109	Cattrysse	79
Alegria	192	Bistro De Tijd	35	Chalet Minigolf	186
Allegria	56	Bistro Mathilda	26	Chalet Westhinder	67
Amadee	195	Bistro Merlot	36	Charlie's Lunchroom	39
Ambrosia	190	Blanches Voiles	208	Chez Marie	78
American House	111	Blankenberge		Chocolaterie Ledoux	40
André Simoens		beach huts	244	Chocolaterie M	40
Gallery	180	Bluepoint	77	Christmas Truce Cross	139
Antique Café	62	Boerenhol	60	Christophorus	175
Ariane	190	Bonne Auberge	209	Ciccio	32
Au Nouveau St-Eloi	60	Brasserie Bristol	36	Cinema Rio	183
Au Palais du Picon	24	Brasserie		Colne Valley Cemetery	110
Au Pinguin	43	Oosterstaketsel	33	Commandobunker	
Au Saumon d'Or	45	Brasserie Rubens	35	Kemmel	220

Cook & Roll 35
Corman 82
Corman by Filigranes 82
Couleur Locale 80
Craters and mines
    walk 130
Crest Farm 126
Cromwell 28
Cuines 33 33
De 12 Apostels 52
De Akkerwinde 195
De Barbier 55
De Blankaart 214
De Concessie 168
De Crayon 65
De Dolle Brouwers 212
De Fonderie 15
De Gevleugelde Stad 218
De Grote Post 181
De Haan tram station 178
De Haan Villas 165
De Helleketel 61
De Ijshoeve 43
De Karavaan 74
De Klaproos 195
De Kloosterloft 201
De Lijn bus 14 103
De Lovie 148
De Maré 63
De Markt 30
De Mikke 34
De Mosselbeurs 29
De Oude Kaasmakerij 47
De Peerdevisscher 38, 244
De Plukker 212
De Rentmeesterhoeve 194

De Ruyffelaer 16
De Stadsschaal 58
De Steenen Haene 17
De Struise Brouwers 213
De Tere Plekke 55
De Voerman 16
De Vrede 22
De Witte Parel 41
Death Cells 100
Découverte 14
Delhy 41
Den Artiest 34
Den Ekster 55
Den Olifant 15
Design Clinic 80
Dodengang 118
Dranouter Folk
    Festival 219
Du Parc 62
Duinbergen Minigolf 187
Dumont Quarter 167
Elverdinge 148
Elzenwalle 147
Ensor House 161
Eton Memorial School 95
Evergreen 206
Fabiaan Van Severen 74
Ferrer 76
Fields of Gold 193
Flanders Battlefield
    Tours 102
Flanders Fields American
    Cemetery 126
Flavie's Tafel 27
Flugplatz Peselhoek 221
Fort Napoleon 33, 220

FRAC 152
Frederic Blondeel 41
Friedhof roggeveld 127
Frontline Tours 103
Galerie Beau Site 75
Galerie Ronny
    Van de Velde 179
Galerie Zwart Huis 179
Garden 128
Gas Attach
    Monument 128
Geukens & De Vil 179
Glacier de la Poste 42
Glamping Ecochique 203
Gossip 56
Grand Cabaret 26
Grand Hôtel Bellevue 166
Haig House 98, 128
Haut Bonheur
    de la Table 23
Hedge Row Trench
    Cemetery 104
Heist lighthouse 177
Hemmingway 69
Het Blauwershof 24
Het Jagershof 61
Het Mysterie 59
Het Ovenhuis 20
Het Schaliënhof 200
Het Zoute 168
Het Zwin 164
Hill 60 130, 131
Hommelhof 19
Hooglede Cemetery 114
Hop Museum 149
Hotel Het Wethuys 197

Hotel Reverie 197
Hotel Skindles 101
Huyze Elimonica 207
Ice Mountain 238
Ieper Strand 99
IJs René 43
In Beveren 60
In de Vrede 54
In de Wulf 19
In de Zon 20
In Flanders
   Fields Museum 83, 88, 91
Irish Tower 126
Island of Ireland
   Peace Park 137
Items 208
Jens Vishandel 44
Kaffee Bazaar 53
Karamel 57
Kasteelhof 't Hooghe 197
Käthe Kollwitz
   Museum 151
Kemmelberg 130, 145
Kijkhut De Zeehond 173
Kombuis 30
Kruisstraat Crater 123
Kusthistories 161
L'Amuzette 75
L'Apereau 68
La Bassecour 115
La Carrefour
   des Roses 139
La Galleria 37
La Passion Interdite 205
La Piscine 153
La Porte Cochère 192

La Poupée 58
LAAC 153
Lafayette Musicbar 65
Lange Max Museum 151
Langemark 90
Lapidarium 95
Last Post Anniversary 249
Le Coup Vert 32
Le vent qui souffle
   où il veut 175
Leeuwenbrug
   sculptures 178
Leopoldpark Minigolf 186
Lifeguards 245
Light Front 1914 248
Lijssenthoek Cemetery 88
Loft Living 81
Lone Tree Cemetery 106, 144
Lone Tree Crater 123
Louise-Marie Chapel 169
Louvre Lens 152
Main Street Hotel 190
Manitoba 205
Manoir Carpe Diem 204
Manoir Ogygia 196
Markt XI 26
Martins Visrestaurant 28
Menen German
   Cemetery 114
Menin Gate 93, 125
Mesen Church Crypt 115
Mimi's 57
Minigolf Petit Pois 187
Monroe Beach 67
MU.zee 183
Musée de Flandre 153

Navigo 162
New Year Swim 245
Nieuwpoort Ferry 173
Nightshop 69
Normandie 177
Notarishuys 21, 198
Nr12 76
Obelisk 76
Oesterput 29
Oosterstaketsel 185
Ostend East Beach 169
Ostend Ferry 174
Oud Vlaenderen 58
Our Lady of the Dunes
   Church 169
Over The Top Tours
   Bookshop 83
Pacific Eiland 17
Palingbeek Nature
   Reserve 129, 144, 214
Parking 174
Passchendaele Memorial
   Museum 90, 118, 238
Patricia Couture 99
Paul Delvaux Museum 181
Pegasus 21
Permeke Museum 183
Philippe Nuyens 25
Pied de Poule 77
Pill Boxes 96
Plassendale 37
Ploegsteert Wood 113, 215
Poedertoren 96
Polygoonbos 215
Poperinge
   Beer Festival 219

Poperinge Old Military
   Cemetery 113
Poseidon 65
Poterne Staircase 97
Predikherentoren 97
Prefectenhuis 207
Puydtjes 46
Ramparts Cemetery 96
Raversijde 221
Recour 196
Red Farm Cemetery 110
Regina 191
Rekhof Cemetery 100
René's
   In de stad Kortrijk 39
Rent a Guide 102
Resto Real 30
Rifle House Cemetery 104
Rock Strangers 176
Rodeberg chair lift 145
Rollywood 79
Rood 69
Roses de vents II 176
Sabbajon 193
Saint-Hubert 54
Saint-Yvon Crater 123
Salient Tours 102
Samuel Vanhoegaerden
   Gallery 180
Sanctuary Wood 118
Sansen 46
Savarin 27
Schildia 66
School Museum 149
Sel Gris 25
Sénégalais Quarter 167

Shell Shock 249
Siesta Beach 66
Sint Rochus Quarter 167
Sint-Bernardus 213
Sint-Eloi Crater 121
Soepboer 245
Souvenir 14
Spanbroekmolen
   Cemetery 106
Spioenkop 184
Sportsman Bar 124
St George's Memorial
   Church 93
St Martin's Cathedral 95
Stadsmuseum
   Oostende 161
Stone Foundations 99
Suffolk Cemetery 109
Suite 17 208
Summer Concerts 174
Talbot House 100, 203
Taverne Koekoek 38
Ter Yde
   Nature Reserve 163
Terminus 20
The Black House 166
The British Grenadier
   Bookshop 83
The Fat Cat 53
The Old House 200
The Pharmacy 68
The Siege of Ypres 221
The Times 52
Tortelbos 239
Trattoria Alloro 15
Twins Club 66

Tyne Cot 90
Uitkerkse polder 170
Van Raemdonck
   Brothers Chapel 112
Varlet Farm 194
Villa Alta 209
Villa D'Hondt 207
Villa des Zéphyrs 165
Villa Elsa 206
Villa La Tourelle 205
Villa Select 204
Villa Vanilla 193
Vishandel De Paepe 45
Vistrap 44
Vladslo Cemetery 106
Vlamertinge 147
Vrijbos 215
Wally's Farm 59
Watou Art Festival 218
Webcams 185
Weeuwhof 101
Welsh Memorial 137
Westhinder 44
White Interiors 80
Ypres City Museum 151
Zandvoorde Bunker 111
Zonnebeke Bikes 78
Zuydcoote beach 170

COLOPHON

EDITING *and* COMPOSING – Derek Blyth

GRAPHIC DESIGN – Joke Gossé

PHOTOGRAPHY – Joram Van Holen and Jonas Mertens

The author and publisher wish to thank Christa Deplacie and Diederik Vandenbilcke, who were consulted regarding the selection of the addresses in this book.

D/2014/12.005/8

ISBN 978 94 6058 1281

NUR 506

© 2014, Luster, Antwerp

www.lusterweb.com

info@lusterweb.com

Printed in Spain by Indice S.L. Arts Gràfiques.